Bloom's
GUIDES

T. S. Eliot's
The Waste Land

The Adventures of Huckleberry Finn

All the Pretty Horses

Animal Farm

Beloved

Beowulf

Brave New World

The Catcher in the Rye

The Chosen

The Crucible

Cry, the Beloved Country

Death of a Salesman

Fahrenheit 451

Frankenstein

The Glass Menagerie

The Grapes of Wrath

Great Expectations

The Great Gatsby

Hamlet

The Handmaid's Tale

The House on Mango Street

I Know Why the Caged Bird Sings

The Iliad

Jane Eyre

Lord of the Flies

Macbeth

Maggie: A Girl of the Streets

The Member of the Wedding

The Metamorphosis

Native Son

Of Mice and Men

1984

The Odyssey

Oedipus Rex

One Hundred Years of Solitude

Pride and Prejudice

Ragtime

The Red Badge of Courage

Romeo and Juliet

Slaughterhouse-Five

The Scarlet Letter

Snow Falling on Cedars

A Streetcar Named Desire

The Sun Also Rises

A Tale of Two Cities

The Things They Carried

To Kill a Mockingbird

The Waste Land

Bloom's
GUIDES

T. S. Eliot's
The Waste Land

Edited & with an Introduction
by Harold Bloom

BLOOM'S
LITERARY CRITICISM
An imprint of Infobase Publishing

Bloom's Guides: The Waste Land

Copyright © 2007 by Infobase Publishing

Introduction © 2007 by Harold Bloom

All rights reserved. No part of this book may be reproduced or utilized in any form or by any means, electronic or mechanical, including photocopying, recording, or by any information storage or retrieval systems, without permission in writing from the publisher. For information contact:

Bloom's Literary Criticism
An imprint of Infobase Publishing
132 West 31st Street
New York, NY 10001

Library of Congress Cataloging-in-Publication Data
T.S. Eliot's The waste land / [edited and with an introduction by] Harold Bloom.
    p. cm. — (Bloom's guides)
Includes bibliographical references (p. 103) and index.
ISBN-13: 978-0-7910-9361-0
ISBN-10: 0-7910-9361-1
    1. Eliot, T. S. (Thomas Stearns), 1888–1965. Waste land. I. Bloom, Harold. II. Title. III. Series.

PS3509.L43W3816 2007
821'.912—dc22   2006101020

Bloom's Literary Criticism books are available at special discounts when purchased in bulk quantities for businesses, associations, institutions, or sales promotions. Please call our Special Sales Department in New York at (212) 967-8800 or (800) 322-8755.

You can find Bloom's Literary Criticism on the World Wide Web at http://www.chelseahouse.com

Contributing Editor: Neil Heims
Cover design by Takeshi Takahashi
Printed in the United States of America
Bang EJB 10 9 8 7 6 5 4 3 2 1
This book is printed on acid-free paper.

All links and web addresses were checked and verified to be correct at the time of publication. Because of the dynamic nature of the web, some addresses and links may have changed since publication and may no longer be valid.

Contents

# Introduction

HAROLD BLOOM

In his essay, "The *Pensées* of Pascal" (1931), Eliot remarked upon Pascal's adversarial relation to his true precursor, Montaigne:

> One cannot destroy Pascal, certainly; but of all authors Montaigne is one of the least destructible. You could as well dissipate a fog by flinging hand-grenades into it. For Montaigne is a fog, a gas, a fluid, insidious element. He does not reason, he insinuates, charms, and influences.

Walt Whitman, too, is "a fluid, insidious element," a poet who "insinuates, charms, and influences." And he is the darkest of poets, despite his brazen self-advertisements and his passionate hopes for his nation. *Song of Myself*, for all its joyous epiphanies, chants also of the waste places:

> Of the turbid pool that lies in the autumn forest,
> Of the moon that descends the steeps of the
>   soughing twilight,
> Toss, sparkles of day and dusk—toss on the
>   black stems that decay in the muck,
> Toss to the moaning gibberish of the dry limbs.

No deep reader of Whitman could forget the vision of total self-rejection that is the short poem, "A Hand-Mirror":

> Hold it up sternly—see this it sends back, (who is
>   it? is it you?)
> Outside fair costume, within ashes and filth,
> No more a flashing eye, no more a sonorous voice
>   or springy step,
> Now some slave's eye, voice, hands, step,

A drunkard's breath, unwholesome eater's face,
    venerealee's flesh,
Lungs rotting away piecemeal, stomach sour and
    cankerous,
Joints rheumatic, bowels clogged with abomination,
Blood circulating dark and poisonous streams,
Words babble, hearing and touch callous,
No brain, no heart left, no magnetism of sex;
Such from one look in this looking-glass ere you go
    hence,
Such a result so soon—and from such a beginning!

Rather than multiply images of despair in Whitman, I turn
to the most rugged of his self-accusations, in the astonishing
"Crossing Brooklyn Ferry":

It is not upon you alone the dark patches fall,
The dark threw its patches down upon me also,
The best I had done seem'd to me blank and suspicious,
My great thoughts as I supposed them, were they not
    in reality meagre?
Nor is it you alone who know what it is to be evil,
I am he who knew what it was to be evil,
I too knotted the old knot of contrariety,
Blabb'd, blush'd, resented, lied, stole, grudg'd,
Had guile, anger, lust, hot wishes I dared not speak,
Was wayward, vain, greedy, shallow, sly, cowardly,
    malignant,
The wolf, the snake, the hog, not wanting in me,
The cheating look, the frivolous word, the adulterous
    wish, not wanting,
Refusals, hates, postponements, meanness, laziness,
    none of these wanting,
Was one with the rest, the days and haps of the rest,
Was call'd by my nighest name by clear loud voices of young
    men as they saw me approaching or passing,
Felt their arms on my neck as I stood, or the negligent
    leaning of their flesh against me as I sat,

Saw many I loved in the street or ferry-boat or public
    assembly, yet never told them a word,
Lived the same life with the rest, the same old
    laughing, gnawing, sleeping,
Play'd the part that still looks back on the actor or
    actress,
The same old role, the role that is what we make it, as
    great as we like,
Or as small as we like, or both great and small.

The barely concealed allusions to Milton's Satan and to *King Lear* strengthen Whitman's catalog of vices and evasions, preparing the poet and his readers for the darker intensities of the great *Sea-Drift* elegies and "Lilacs," poems that are echoed everywhere in Eliot's verse, but particularly in "The Death of Saint Narcissus," *The Waste Land*, and "The Dry Salvages." Many critics have charted these allusions, but I would turn consideration of Eliot's agon with Whitman to the question: "Why Whitman?" It is poetically unwise to go down to the waterline, or go to the headland with Walt Whitman, for then the struggle takes place in an arena where the poet who found his identifying trope in the sea-drift cannot lose.

An answer must be that the belated poet does not choose his trial by landscape or seascape. It is chosen for him by his precursor. Browning's quester in "Childe Roland to the Dark Tower Came" is as overdetermined by Shelley as Eliot is overdetermined by Whitman in *The Waste Land*, which is indeed Eliot's version of "Childe Roland," as it is Eliot's version of Percivale's quest in Tennyson's "The Holy Grail," a poem haunted by Keats in the image of Galahad. "Lilacs" is everywhere in *The Waste Land*: in the very lilacs bred out of the dead land, in the song of the hermit thrush in the pine trees, and most remarkably in the transumption of Whitman walking down to where the hermit thrush sings, accompanied by two companions walking beside him, the thought of death and the knowledge of death:

Then with the knowledge of death as walking one
    side of me,

And the thought of death close-walking the other
    side of me,
And I in the middle as with companions, and as
    holding the hands of companions,
I fled forth to the hiding receiving night that talks
    not,
Down to the shores of the water, the path by the
    swamp in the dimness,
To the solemn shadowy cedars and ghostly pines so
    still.

The "crape-veil'd women" singing their dirges through
the night for Lincoln are hardly to be distinguished from
Eliot's "murmur of maternal lamentation," and Whitman's
"tolling tolling bells' perpetual clang" goes on tolling
reminiscent bells in *The Waste Land* as it does in "The
Dry Salvages." Yet all this is only a first-level working of
the influence process, of interest mostly as a return of the
repressed. Deeper, almost beyond analytical modes as yet
available to criticism, is Eliot's troubled introjection of his
nation's greatest and inescapable elegiac poet. "Lilacs" has
little to do with the death of Lincoln but everything to do
with Whitman's ultimate poetic crisis, beyond which his
strongest poetry will cease. *The Waste Land* has little to
do with neo-Christian polemics concerning the decline of
Western culture, and everything to do with a poetic crisis
that Eliot could not quite surmount, in my judgment, since I
do not believe that time will confirm the estimate that most
contemporary critics have made of *Four Quartets*.

The decisive moment or negative epiphany of Whitman's
elegy centers upon his giving up of the tally, the sprig of
lilac that is the synecdoche for his image of poetic voice,
which he yields up to death and to the hermit thrush's song of
death. Eliot's parallel surrender in "What the Thunder Said"
is to ask "what have we given?," where the implicit answer
is "a moment's surrender," a negative moment in which the
image of poetic voice is achieved only as one of Whitman's
"retrievements out of the night."

In his essay on Pascal, Eliot says of Montaigne, a little resentfully but with full accuracy, that "he succeeded in giving expression to the skepticism of *every* human being," presumably including Pascal, and Shakespeare, and even T. S. Eliot. What did Whitman succeed in expressing with equal universality? Division between "myself" and "the real me" is surely the answer. Walt Whitman, one of the roughs, an American, is hardly identical with "the Me myself" who:

> Looks with its sidecurved head curious what will come
> next,
> Both in and out of the game, and watching and
> wondering at it.

Thomas Stearns Eliot, looking with side-curved head, both in and out of the game, has little in common with Walt Whitman, one of the roughs, an American, yet almost can be identified with that American "Me myself."

II

The line of descent from Shelley and Keats through Browning and Tennyson to Pound and Eliot would be direct were it not for the intervention of the genius of the shores of America, the poet of *Leaves of Grass*. Whitman enforces upon Pound and Eliot the American difference, which he had inherited from Emerson, the fountain of our eloquence and of our pragmatism. Most reductively defined, the American poetic difference ensues from a sense of acute isolation, both from an overwhelming space of natural reality and from an oppressive temporal conviction of belatedness, of having arrived after the event. The inevitable defense against nature is the Gnostic conviction that one is no part of the creation, that one's freedom is invested in the primal abyss. Against belatedness, defense involves an immersion in allusiveness, hardly for its own sake, but in order to reverse the priority of the cultural, pre-American past. American poets from Whitman and Dickinson onwards are more like Milton than Milton is,

11

and so necessarily they are more profoundly Miltonic than even Keats or Tennyson was compelled to be.

What has wasted the land of Eliot's elegiac poem is neither the malady of the Fisher King nor the decline of Christianity, and Eliot's own psychosexual sorrows are not very relevant either. The precursors' strength is the illness of *The Waste Land*; Eliot after all can promise to show us "fear in a handful of dust" only because the monologist of Tennyson's *Maud* already has cried out: "Dead, long dead, / Long dead! / And my heart is a handful of dust." Even more poignantly, Eliot is able to sum up all of Whitman's extraordinary "As I Ebb'd with the Ocean of Life" in the single line: "These fragments I have shored against my ruins," where the fragments are not only the verse paragraphs that constitute the text of *The Waste Land*, but crucially are also Whitman's floating sea-drift:

Me and mine, loose windrows, little corpses,
Froth, snowy white, and bubbles,
(See, from my dead lips the ooze exuding at last,
See, the prismatic colors glistening and rolling,)
Tufts of straw, sands, fragments,
Buoy'd hither from many moods, one contradicting
    another.
From the storm, the long calm, the darkness, the swell,
Musing, pondering, a breath, a briny tear, a dab of
    liquid or soil,
Up just as much out of fathomless workings fermented
    and thrown,
A limp blossom or two, torn, just as much over waves
    floating, drifted at random,
Just as much for us that sobbing dirge of Nature,
Just as much whence we come that blare of the cloud—
    trumpets,
We, capricious, brought hither we know not whence,
    spread out before you,
You up there walking or sitting,
Whoever you are, we too lie in drifts at your feet.

"Tufts of straw, sands, fragments" are literally "shored" against Whitman's ruins, as he wends "the shores I know," the shores of America to which, Whitman said, Emerson had led all of us, Eliot included. Emerson's essays, Eliot pugnaciously remarked, "are already an encumbrance," and so they were, and are, and evermore must be for an American writer, but inescapable encumbrances are also stimuli, as Pascal learned in regard to the overwhelming Montaigne.

Biographical Sketch

Thomas Stearns Eliot, the youngest of seven children, was born in St. Louis, Missouri, on September 26, 1888. His father, Henry Ware Eliot, was the president of the Hydraulic Press Brick Company. His mother, Charlotte Champe Stearns, had been a teacher and wrote poetry. Eliot's paternal grandfather, William Greenleaf Eliot, after graduating from the Harvard Divinity School, went west and settled in St. Louis, where he established the city's Unitarian Church. Nevertheless, the family's roots remained in Massachusetts, where they spent each summer. In 1886, Henry Eliot built a house at Eastern Point in Gloucester.

Eliot grew up in two contrasting geographies and cultures. The neighborhood in St. Louis in which the Eliots lived was in decline, but because of their ties to the city, they did not move to the suburbs as others of their class did. Thus Eliot was familiar with the rundown streets of the city and the well-to-do drawing rooms of his parents' social circle. Similarly, although he was raised Unitarian, his nurse, Annie Dunne, an Irish Catholic, sometimes took him to Mass. These conflicting influences are apparent in Eliot's poetry, especially in *The Waste Land*, where high and low dialects, popular and classical culture, and upper and lower class characters are juxtaposed.

In 1905, Eliot left St. Louis and Smith Academy to spend his last year before college at Milton Academy outside Boston. In 1906, he entered Harvard, where the intellectual and cultural foundation of his poetry was laid. In his first year, Eliot was put on academic probation for poor grades, but he went on to complete his B.A. in three years and earned an M.A. the fourth. Among his teachers were the philosopher George Santayana and Irving Babbitt, an influential literary scholar and culture critic whose conservative moral thought generated a movement called the New Humanism. With Santayana he studied allegory and read Dante in Italian; Babbit introduced him to Eastern religion, Sanskrit, and French literary criticism. Both teachers influenced Eliot's own austere political and moral conservatism.

In 1909, in the Harvard library, Eliot came across Arthur Symons' book, *The Symbolist Movement in Literature*, where he discovered the work of the French poet, Jules Laforgue, which exerted paramount influence in shaping the tone of Eliot's early poetry, including "The Love Song of J. Alfred Prufrock." At Harvard, too, Eliot met the English philosopher and mathematician, Bertrand Russell. In 1910, Eliot joined the staff of the literary magazine, *The Harvard Advocate*. Within the circle of its contributors, he broadened his knowledge of contemporary poets and poetry, including the poetry of Ezra Pound, who would shape *The Waste Land*. He also met the poet and novelist, Conrad Aiken, then a fellow student, who would remain a life-long friend and who introduced him later, in London, to Pound.

Eliot spent the year after graduation in 1910 living near the Sorbonne in Paris and attending classes in French literature. He also attended the lectures of the philosopher Henri Bergson at the *College de France*. At his lodgings, he developed a close friendship with Jean Verdenal, one of his neighbors, a medical student who was killed in the First World War and to whom Eliot dedicated "The Love Song of J. Alfred Prufrock." Before returning to the United States in 1911, Eliot traveled through Italy and Germany and visited London. He had also composed a number of his famous early poems including "Prufrock," "Portrait of a Lady," "Rhapsody on a Windy Night," "Preludes," and "La Figlia che Piange."

Back at Harvard in 1911, Eliot began doctoral studies in philosophy under a group of such distinguished philosophers as Santayana, William James, Josiah Royce, Bertrand Russell, and F. H. Bradley, who directed his thesis on Bergson. Also at this time, he taught undergraduate courses in philosophy. Eliot led a lively social life in Boston. He appeared in theatricals, took dancing and skating lessons, attended concerts, and began a romance with Emily Hale that seemed to be leading to marriage until he abruptly broke it off in 1914 when he returned to Europe, first traveling through Germany, Belgium, and Holland, but, with the start of the First World War, settling in England.

In London, during the summer of 1914, Eliot showed Conrad Aiken, his friend from Harvard, some of his poems, and Aiken showed them to Pound, who recommended them enthusiastically to Harriet Monroe, now the legendary editor of *Poetry* magazine. In June 1915, "Prufrock" appeared in *Poetry*. "Preludes" and "Rhapsody on a Windy Night" appeared in *Blast*, a magazine edited by the novelist and painter Wyndham Lewis, in July. Later that year, "Portrait of a Lady" was published by the avant-garde poet and editor Alfred Kreymborg in *Others*. Eliot was granted admission to an elite circle of writers, painters, editors, and patrons all dedicated to modernity. At this time, Eliot was also enrolled at Merton College, Oxford, studying Aristotle and, with Bertrand Russell, logic.

In 1915, Eliot married Vivienne Haigh-Wood. It was a disastrous marriage that began badly. Vivienne was an exuberant and high-strung woman with a taste for gaiety and an appreciation of Eliot's poetry. His family opposed their apparently impulsive wedding. Worse, Eliot was unable to consummate their union and from the start of their marriage they slept separately. Because they were poor, Eliot accepted Bertrand Russell's offer that they share his flat. Soon, however, frustrated by a lack of affection from her husband, Vivienne allowed herself to begin a relationship with Russell, of which Eliot was jealous but also tolerant. When Russell broke off the affair with Vivienne in 1918, it shattered her. By that time, too, Eliot had grown colder to her, and her continuing affairs with other men repulsed him. His entrance into the Anglican Church, in 1927, sealed his determination to separate from her, and in the autumn of 1932, when he was invited to deliver the Charles Eliot Norton Lectures on Poetry at Harvard, he left for Cambridge without her. In February 1933, from the United States, he ordered his solicitor in London to serve Vivienne with separation papers, and from that time until her death in 1947, he refused to see her. Distraught and confused, Vivienne was considered mad and was confined by her brother, with Eliot's permission, to a mental institution in 1938, after she had been found wandering around the streets one morning at five a.m. She died in 1947. In 1957, Eliot married Valerie Fletcher, his secretary and forty years his junior. Their marriage was apparently a happy one.

In 1916, Eliot completed his doctoral thesis for Harvard but did not get his degree because he would not return to Harvard to defend the thesis. He tried to earn a living by teaching school, reviewing for magazines, and serving as the assistant editor on a magazine called the *Egoist*. In that capacity, he proofread James Joyce's *Ulysses*, which the *Egoist* was publishing in installments. In 1917, however, he was hired to work in the foreign section of Lloyds Bank, where he remained for nine years until 1926, when Geoffrey Faber hired Eliot as a literary editor for his new publishing company, Faber and Gwyer (which became Faber and Faber).

While he was establishing himself as a poet, Eliot cemented his reputation as one of the most important literary and cultural critics of his era with the publication of a collection of essays in *The Sacred Wood*. Public fame and private distress went hand in hand. In 1919, his father died before he and his son were reconciled over Eliot's emigration and marriage, and in 1921, after a visit to his mother, Eliot suffered a nervous breakdown and spent three months in a sanitarium in Switzerland. In Switzerland, Eliot worked on *The Waste Land*. In Paris, he showed it to Pound, who cut it into the poem it now is. Schofield Thayer, a friend of Eliot's from Harvard, at this time was editing *The Dial*, a literature and arts magazine. In 1921, he established the yearly Dial Awards of $2000 and in 1922, he gave it to Eliot even before he saw the poem. He printed the poem as the centerpiece of the magazine. The poem caused a sensation with its modernist blend of jazzy erudition, disjunction, and despair.

At the height of his fame, in 1922, Eliot was offered the editorship of a magazine of his own by Lady Rothermere, the wife of the publisher of the *Daily Mail*. As the editor of the *Criterion* from 1922 until its final issue in 1939, just before the start of World War Two, Eliot exerted a powerful influence on poetry and thought. He published articles and the poems "The Hollow Men," in 1925, and "Ash Wednesday," in 1930, the poem that reflected his entrance into the Anglican Communion in 1927. From 1936 to 1942, Eliot wrote the "Four Quartets," a series of four poems whose subject is the philosophical consideration of time, reality, experience, and salvation. In 1948, he was awarded the Nobel Prize for Literature.

In addition to poetry and criticism, Eliot wrote verse drama. Perhaps the best known is *The Cocktail Party*, a mixture of Euripides and Noel Coward, which had a successful Broadway run in the early 1950s. His other plays include *The Family Reunion*, a modern version of Aeschylus' *Eumenides*; *Murder in the Cathedral*, about Thomas Beckett; a jazz play in fragments called *Sweeny Agonistes*; *The Confidential Clerk*; and *The Elder Statesman*.

During the final years of his life, Eliot produced little. After his death, his once monumental reputation began to decline, in part because his conservative, monarchist, and sometimes anti-Semitic outlook became less acceptable than it had been before the rise of German fascism, and simply because taste in literature changes with cultural and social changes. Nevertheless, Eliot's critical influence is established and so is his place as a poet. If he is no longer the principal English-language poet of the twentieth century, he is still among the chief poets of the first half of that century, the foremost of those who reshaped poetry and made it new.

The Story Behind the Story

The Waste Land was published in October 1922, in *The Criterion*, the magazine Eliot himself edited in England until he closed it in 1939 on the eve of the Second World War. The poem's first American publication was in *The Dial*, a few weeks later. The poem was a sensation even before it appeared in print. Eliot had been writing sections of *The Waste Land* since his days at Harvard. The poet Conrad Aiken, a fellow student at Harvard and a life-long friend, reported that he remembered the lines, "A woman drew her long black hair out tight/ And fiddled whisper music on those strings," from the fifth section of the poem, from their student days. The fourth section of the poem, "Death by Water," is in large part an English translation of Eliot's poem in French, *"Dans le Restaurant,"* published in 1920. Eliot began work on *The Waste Land* in earnest in 1919. Much of the work was done late in 1921 while Eliot was staying on the coast of Margate in England and then at a sanitarium in Lausanne, Switzerland, where he was taking a rest cure after suffering a nervous breakdown, following the death of his father in 1919 and a visit, during the summer of 1921, to his mother and sister in St. Louis.

When Eliot passed through Paris on the way to Lausanne and on the way back to London from Lausanne, he and his wife Vivienne stayed with Ezra Pound and his wife, Dorothy. Pound looked at the poem on both occasions, and on the second, sharply edited it, cutting away half of it and making suggestions about the half that remained—essentially creating from Eliot's raw material the poem published in 1922. Pound's praise for the poem before it was completed gave it a buzz, which extended to Eliot's friend from Harvard, Schofield Thayer. Thayer edited *The Dial*, published in Boston. One of *The Dial*'s goals was to promote American writers and to extend the influence of American writing. With those goals in mind, Thayer had established the Dial Awards in 1921. Without having seen a finished draft of *The Waste Land*, Thayer named Eliot the recipient of the 1922 Dial Award and planned to make the poem the principal work in the November issue of the magazine.

When *The Waste Land* appeared it was met with the excitement its promoters had hoped would accompany it. Its spirit is one familiar in the period between the two world wars: the disgust and despair with everything that haunted the survivors of what Gertrude Stein called "the lost generation." The grim war behind them served as a harrowing commentary on the empty lives and venal pursuits they saw all around them. Its style suggested the new experiments with structure, continuity, and point of view that were visible in the paintings of Picasso and Braque and in such literary works as the stories of Gertrude Stein, James Joyce's *Ulysses*, and the novels of Virginia Woolf. In addition, *The Waste Land* combined overwhelming erudition with common, even debased speech. Woven into one fabric were quotations in a number of languages from the great literatures of the world, and from pop songs and the music hall. The jumps from section to section, however, caused some readers to wonder if the threads of the poem really constituted one fabric. To add to the complexity and impenetrability of the poem, when it appeared in book form, Eliot added footnotes. They often are as obscure as the poem itself, increasing the scope of difficulty and suggesting the breadth of literary, philosophical, anthropological, and religious scholarship the poem seems to demand.

In 1922, Eliot sent the original manuscript drafts of *The Waste Land*, the version of the poem that existed before Pound edited it, to John Quinn in New York City. Quinn was a lawyer whose avocation was collecting manuscripts, particularly of the Modernist writers. He also was the source of the $2000 attached to the Dial Award granted to Eliot in 1922. When he died in 1924, his daughter, Julia Anderson, inherited his papers and kept them in storage. To the literary world and to Eliot scholars, the original drafts of *The Waste Land* seemed to be lost. In 1953, John Flick, a visitor to the home of Julia Anderson's daughter, Mary Conroy, to whom she had left her father's papers, noticed the manuscript on a bookshelf.

Although the Conroys were aware of it and of what it was, they had never given it much thought. Encouraged by Flick, the Conroys decided to give the manuscript and many other papers in John Quinn's collection to the New York Public Library. They started cataloguing the papers and in the early sixties began sending them from their home in California to John Gordan, the curator of the library's Berg Collection. Gordan, out of respect for Eliot, who was still alive, did not make the acquisition or the existence of the manuscript public until Eliot died in 1965. Then Gordan sent a microfilm of the manuscript to Valerie Fletcher Eliot, Eliot's widow and his secretary, and she put together an edition of the original drafts. It was published as *The Waste Land: Facsimile and Manuscripts of the Original Drafts* in 1971.

Just as the complete manuscript drafts of *The Waste Land* made clearer the meaning and the method of the poem, so, too, have the biographical details of Eliot's married and emotional life in the late teens and early 1920s helped to clarify certain aspects of the poem. Even though Eliot was known to have said that the poem represented his own grumblings rather than a serious social critique, his primary aesthetic principle of literature, that the poet should remove himself from his work, made his observation seem like a tease rather than a serious comment. Biographical scholarship emerging at the end of the twentieth century, however, has focused on the unhappiness of his first marriage, particularly on his own sexual impotence and his wife's nervous agitation and sexual promiscuity. These factors illuminate, even while not entirely accounting for, the personalities of the narrator and of the woman in the first part of "A Game of Chess"—his diffidence and her high-strung sensuality. Similarly, the intensity of Eliot's friendship with Jean Verdenal, who was killed in 1915 in the war, in Paris in 1911 may have affected the composition of "Death by Water" and the mournful tone of the poem as a whole. Eliot used the circumstances and the emotions of his own life to invent and give vitality to images which were partially drawn from his own experiences and yet reflected a world broader than his own private one.

List of Characters

The Cumaean Sibyl appears in the epigram at the head of the poem. A guest at a Roman feast in the satirical novel by Petronius, c. 27–66 A.D., *The Satyricon*, relates her story. Granted eternal life by Apollo, she neglected to ask also for eternal youth and lived a life in death, continually withering but never dying.

Ezra Pound, American poet, author of *The Cantos*, edited *The Waste Land*, cutting it in half and giving it the shape and texture that define it as the ground-breaking work it is. In recognition of his craftsmanship, Eliot dedicated the poet to him, using the Italian inscription translated as "the better craftsman."

The poet narrator recites the poem, assuming many voices. In his own voice, he seems to be an intellectual and ineffectual man, tormented by a sense that history has run down, civilization has decayed and that culture, while comforting to his lonely soul, describes the failures and torments of mankind but cannot bring salvation.

Marie is the poet's first interlocutor. She tells him over coffee of her past in Austria and of her cousin, who was the Archduke Rudolph, the heir to the Austro-Hungarian throne and how she used to go sledding in the mountains.

Isolde, the heroine of Richard Wagner's opera *Tristan und Isolde*, is referred to in the quotation from the opera beginning at line 31. She falls desperately in love with Tristan, who had been sent by his king, Mark, to bring her back to him as a bride. Tristan falls in love with her, too, after they drink a love potion.

Madame Sosostris is a clairvoyant and tarot card reader, a fortune teller. As she turns over the cards in her deck, she introduces several of the characters present in the poem through allusion:

The drowned Phoenician sailor refers to Phlebas the Phoenician, whose death is the subject of the "Death by Water" section of the poem.

The man with three staves, Eliot states in his notes, he associates with the Fisher King, the impotent ruler of the waste land, and the prevailing spirit of *The Waste Land*.

The one-eyed merchant is a figure that may be associated with Mr. Eugenides, the Smyrna merchant in the third section of the poem who propositions the narrator.

The Hanged Man, Eliot says, he associates with the dying god and with the hooded figure in the last section of the poem, that is with Jesus as he was after his resurrection, when he appeared to some of his disciples on their way to Emmaus.

Stetson is a figure the narrator encounters on London Bridge, representing survivors of war.

"She" is the way Eliot identifies the wealthy and nervous woman in the richly appointed salon that begins the second section of the poem.

Cleopatra, the hot-tempered and volatile Egyptian queen, as she is portrayed in Shakespeare's *Antony and Cleopatra*, is present by allusion as a precursor spirit to the woman Eliot refers to as "she," because her chair is compared to Cleopatra's barge on the Nile.

Tereus and **Philomela** are pictured over the mantelpiece. In the *Metamorphoses*, Ovid tells the story of how Tereus raped his wife's sister, Philomela, and how he was changed into a hawk and she into a swallow.

Gossip in a dive is an unidentified cockney women who tells the story of:

23

Lil, a woman who has had five children and an abortion and is old beyond her years. She would like to break off sexual relations with her husband.

Lil's husband is returning from the army and, according to the **Gossip,** will be looking for "a good time" with another woman if his wife is unavailable.

Barman calls out that the bar is closing as the **Gossip** tells her tale.

Ophelia is the young woman used by her father and spurned by Hamlet in Shakespeare's play, who dies by drowning. In the poem, the goodnights the bar patrons exchange segue into her last words in *Hamlet*.

Mrs. Porter is the keeper of a brothel in a bawdy song from which Eliot quotes.

Her daughter is one of her prostitutes.

Sweeney, one of her clients, is a recurring figure in Eliot's poetry and represents a rather degenerate example of the human species, governed by lust and greed.

Mr. Eugenides is the merchant referred to by Madame Sosostris. He propositions the narrator.

Tiresias, to whom the poet compares himself and who, Eliot explains is his notes, represents the point at which all the characters in the poem converge, is a character from Ovid's *Metamorphoses* who existed serially as both male and female. In his final embodiment as a male he was blind but had the power of prophecy.

The Typist lives in a small bed-sitter.

The Clerk is a vain young man who visits her.

The Rhine Maidens, the spirits of the Rhine River from Richard Wagner's Ring Cycle, are parodied as **Thames Maidens,** the spirit of the Thames.

Queen Elizabeth I and her favorite, **Leicester,** are imagined on the Thames, contrasting the opulence of the Renaissance with the industrial waste of Eliot's time.

Saint Augustine, an early Church Father, is alluded to in the line referring to Carthage. Augustine wrote *The Confessions* in which he tells of his conversion from a dissolute youth to a life of religious asceticism.

The Buddha's sermon in which he spoke of everything being on fire is referred to in the repetition of the word "burning."

Roman soldiers are suggested by the allusion to "torchlight red on sweaty faces" in the final section of the poem, which presents the capture, crucifixion, and resurrection of **Jesus** in a series of images and allusions.

The thunder is personified and made to speak the words of **Prajapati,** the Hindu God of creation.

The Prince of Aquitaine is a character in a poem by Gerard de Nerval, an early nineteenth-century French poet whom Eliot quotes. The prince, like the poet/narrator, laments the fallen glory of his condition by using the image of a fallen tower.

Hieronymo is a character in the Elizabethan revenge tragedy, **The Spanish Tragedy,** by Thomas Kyd. Eliot's allusion suggests the vicissitudes of his own emotional condition when caught between the despair engendered in him by the waste land around him and within himself, and the as-yet-unrealizable possibility of salvation.

Summary and Analysis

I.

"What are the roots that clutch?" This is the central question of *The Waste Land*. A challenge delivered at line 19 of the poem, it states directly the problem the poem confronts throughout its five cryptic, fragmented sections. Before Eliot begins to answer the question at the end of line 20, he asks another, related one. "[W]hat branches grow out of this stony rubbish?" Using the images, "branches" and "stony rubbish," he suggests that the poem will examine people's lives (branches) and the culture (stony rubbish) in which they live. By yoking these two images, Eliot shows their interconnection. How can "branches grow" if "roots" cannot "clutch" because the soil is "stony rubbish?" How can people live well if the culture is broken, harsh, and cannot support them? Or, just as troubling, what sort of "branches" can "grow" in a barren culture? How can there be a civilization worthy of mankind and how can mankind itself be whole, wholesome, and create a worthy culture, if the environment in which it grows undermines life rather than nurtures it? The branches that do grow, what sort of branches can they be? The lives that are lived, what kind of lives can they be? As a quest for a way out of the waste land of the world of the early twentieth century, *The Waste Land* is a description of that territory, and of the people who live in it and the quality of the lives they live.

The answer to the question "What are the roots that clutch?" begins on the same line the question ends. In the question there is a suggestion of what the answer must reveal. The problem the question implicitly establishes is "How can rootlessness or uprootedness be repaired?" There must be a nourishing ground to which the roots may clutch so that the branches may grow. The answer the poem first provides seems of little help. "Son of man,/ You cannot say, or guess." It is a simple answer: "You" do not know the answer. "You" are without roots and "you" do not know what might serve for roots. There is a puzzle, a riddle, a problem which must be solved. There is a mystery which must be encountered. Eliot encountered it and accepted it soon after *The Waste Land* with his entry into the Anglican Church—he abandoned the quest in favor of submission to faith. Eliot decided, as he wrote in 1930, in *Ash Wednesday*, that "Because I do not hope to turn again," he would not "mourn/ The vanished power of the usual reign."

Before this epiphany, still in quest of meaning and not knowing where to turn, in *The Waste Land*, Eliot pictures the problem of the alienated, damaged, and lost person, living in a wasted world and finding nothing: "What are the *roots* that *clutch*, what *branches grow/* Out of this *stony rubbish*?" He seeks the answer in a similarly imagistic form and in a form that is—because of the condition asserted in the question—necessarily fragmented. All the poet has to gather an answer from are fragments. The segmented, cubist-like, body of the poem is the result. The fragmentation of the poem reflects the fragmentation the poet experiences—the fragmentation of the human consciousness, of human faith, of the time and of the culture in which the poet lives. Eliot explores the problem by examining it in three different environments, among the upper classes, among the lower classes, and in the consciousness of the pilgrim-poet seeking the mystery that can restore wholeness and turn the waste land into a fertile soil. Eliot enters into the fragmented regions of the poem and into these personae by using a number of narrative voices differentiated by the variety of dictions found in the poem. In addition, a number of other poetic voices and allusions from other works thread through the poem. Allusive scraps from Baudelaire, Wagner, Spenser, Marvell, ragtime, Shakespeare, and Buddhist texts invest the malaise Eliot is defining with breadth of field and depth of focus. These allusions are transformed by their context into resonances of the alienation Eliot anatomizes.

"You know only," the poet asserts, "a heap of broken images." Images, not meanings, are all that is known. They are "broken images" like the images in the cubist paintings of the artists whose work is contemporary with his, Braque, Leger, and Picasso. In their work, the image that makes up the picture plane no longer resembles a coherent and organized representation of something recognizable and meaningful. Cubist painting presents a decomposed re-organization of apparently incoherently arranged shards of things no longer congruent with everyday perception. In a world that does not make sense, how can a picture of that world, if it is to be an accurate representation, make sense? The images in those paintings and in Eliot's poem reflect and represent odd and oddly juxtaposed planes of being and experience, which challenge our ability to make sense of what we see. From the images that the poet gathers in *The Waste Land* in a series of fragments, the reader may, like the poet, deduce their insufficiency. The poet guides the reader through a world and through a search for meaning, coherence, for something upon which to rely. To begin to find meaning, the poet must guide the reader outside that world, as he does in the fifth section when he abandons western values for eastern ones. Before attempting to find an answer, however, the poet must lead readers through an experience that demonstrably convinces them that the problem he decries—that the want of solidity, the utter meaninglessness and rootlessness that he encounters— really exists.

The Waste Land is a riddle the reader must unravel in the quest to find "roots that clutch" and something that is more than "a heap of broken images." Yet, at the end of the poem, the poet declares the quest has not quite been successful: "These fragments I have shored against my ruins." They are not entirely worthless, but they are, still and all, fragments, nothing solid, "stony rubbish" from which nothing can grow rather than a rock upon which to build. And there are ruins, the poet's ruins, the edifice of himself that is no longer whole, perhaps identical to the edifice of a culture which stands only in decay. The fragments, the broken images are the remains of something that was once, presumably, solid but is now in ruins. The poet sees himself as a fragmented man, as ruins not reconstituted but "shored up," supported in his ruined condition and kept from crumbling entirely by the fragments he has gathered in the poem.

Between the poet's first mention of "broken images" and his last mention of "fragments," he assembles a number of fragments and broken images which constitute the poem. *The Waste Land* presents itself to the reader as the remains of a poem rather than as a complete poem, just as the culture and the world it describes are only the remains of a culture and of a world. *The Waste Land* as T. S. Eliot presented it to Ezra Pound to look at, is not the poem which was printed in 1922. Pound tore that original apart and struck out large sections of it. What then began as a work that challenged the unity of an ordered structure in its several sections, written in a multiplicity of dialects, dictions, and meters, became a fragment of itself, decomposed and left standing, deliberate ruins with gaping spaces for the reader to look through and beyond.

II.

The Waste Land presents itself immediately as a difficult poem, blocking entrance with an epigraph in Latin and Greek followed by a dedication in Italian. The dedication to Pound, calls him "the better craftsman." The epigram, from the *Satyricon* of Petronius, alludes to the Cumaean Sibyl, the seer who was granted a wish by Apollo and asked for immortality. She neglected to ask for eternal youth. Her immortality thus became a process of continual increased debilitation, and her wish became a longing to die. Her condition reflects the condition of the civilization Eliot leads the reader through in *The Waste Land*, a culture of living death.

The Waste Land begins without any narrative explanation, setting of scene, or introduction of speaker—without the kind of helpful introduction Eliot provided, for example, in his earlier poem, "Portrait of a Lady," which opens with the lines, "Among the smoke and fog of a December afternoon/ You have the scene arrange itself." Eliot begins in the manner of one of Robert Browning's dramatic monologues. Someone is speaking. Who? Or are there more speakers than *one*? The reader does not know.

The first line, "April is the cruellest month," takes hold of the reader and does not let go. It is a simple and a baffling assertion. It grips not because of an implicit reference to or an apparent contradiction of the famous Chaucerian glorification of April with its sweet showers at the beginning of *The Canterbury Tales*. Or even because of the possible suggestion that as we read *The Waste Land*, we, too, like the characters in Chaucer's poem, are setting out on a pilgrimage in search of a martyr who may give life meaning. It astonishes because it is such a simple and apparently false assertion that it makes the reader wonder, why?

"April is the cruellest month" the poet asserts because, he explains by an image, it *breeds* lilacs out of the dead land; it brings life. Implicit is the suggestion that it would be better to allow death to be final. But April undoes death by reinstating life. What then is there about life that should make it undesirable? The answer is that the process of revivification *mixes* memory and desire. It causes the past and the future to clash with each other in the as-yet-unformed and just-beginning present. This juxtaposition has the effect of provoking longing. It *stirs* dull roots with spring rain. Paradoxically, "Winter kept us warm" because it *covers* "Earth in forgetful snow" and *feeds* "A little life with dried tubers." It seems that winter is as close as one can get to death while still alive. It allows, if not death, at least hibernation. Spring, in these lines, rather than being glorious and full of hope, is a cause for alarm. The stirring of life in an environment antithetical to life is painful. Dead winter nourishes without arousing.

These seven lines form the overture of the poem, introducing its themes. "Breeding," "mixing," and "stirring," all disturbing life processes, are highlighted by their placement as the words ending the first three lines of the poem. This introduction culminates in the final word of the fourth line, highlighted by the fact that it is not a present participle, "rain." But rain, here celebrated by its terminal-line placement, will be the one element missing and longed for throughout the body of the poem. Lines 5 and 6 again end in present participles, the more comforting "covering" and "feeding." The section ends

30

with tubers, the buried food that just sustains the hibernation until threatening life bursts forth again.

The overture slides into the first scene with the introduction of a new speaker who is no longer the poet but an aristocratic lady named Marie. The transition is smoothed by the continuing reference to the characteristics of the seasons. From an imagistic exposition, the poem moves to narrative.

> Summer surprised us, coming over the Starnbergersee
> With a shower of rain; we stopped in the colonnade,
> And went on in sunlight, into the Hofgarten,
> And drank coffee, and talked for an hour.

The abstract "us" of the fifth line now refers to the poet/speaker and Marie, with whom he has a cup of coffee and who takes over as the voice of the poem at line 12 with an assertion of her pedigree: "I am not Russian. I come from Lithuania, pure German." And then Marie begins to reminisce:

> When we were children, staying at the arch-duke's,
> My cousin's, he took me out on a sled,
> And I was frightened. He said, Marie,
> Marie, hold on tight. And down we went.
> In the mountains, there you feel free.
> I read, much of the night, and go south in the winter.

Taken literally, this fragment of a conversation Eliot actually had with Countess Marie Larisch, niece of the Austro-Hungarian Empress and cousin of the Austro-Hungarian Crown Prince Rudolph—who killed his mistress and himself at his castle in Mayerling under murky circumstances in 1889—reflects her regret at a lost world. Marie had been the lovers' go-between and was disgraced after their death when her role was discovered. But her words suggest the spiritual condition of the era: the malaise described in the overture. Implicit in "When we were children" is a fatal strain of nostalgia. "We" are no longer children with cousins who are archdukes; the Austro-Hungarian Empire was destroyed in the cataclysmic

First World War. The joy of abandonment when the thrill of rushing downhill in the mountains through the snow on a sled is all the sensation there is, and the fright that comes can be overcome simply by "hold[ing] on tight" is a lost delight. To reflect that "In the mountains, there you feel free," indicates that "you" are oppressed now with a sense of not being free and have, in consequence, withdrawn from the world of experience to the world of contemplation, "read[ing] much of the night, and go[ing] south in winter."

The question, "What are the roots that clutch?" cuts into this scene as a commentary upon it as well as a universal, overwhelming question. Here is rootlessness. In this reflective recitative between the arias, Eliot presents the landscape of the wasteland. It is a terrain "where the sun beats, /And the dead tree gives no shelter, the cricket no relief, /And the dry stone no sound of water." The third in this string of images alludes to the miracle in the desert when Moses, leading the Children of Israel out of Egypt and into the promised land, struck a rock and brought forth in the arid terrain a gush of water. By contrast, only a waste land, not a promised land, extends before us. Additionally, although God is often represented as light, as in the opening of the third book of John Milton's epic poem, *Paradise Lost*, light here is presented not as an illumination but as a presence that scorches and makes a desert. The sun beats and there is not even the sound of water no less water itself. Eliot offers the picture of a present where neither past nor future can relieve the intensity of its barrenness. The present, consequently, is a terrain free from April's cruelty: there is neither memory nor desire. "Only," the poet indicates, there is a sort of relief, but not of a nourishing sort. Relief lies "under the shadow of this red rock." If one follows the speaker's invitation to "Come in under the shadow of this red rock," then there is something to be seen, something horrifying—an image representing the modern world the poem is attempting to conjure up and from which it is attempting to separate the reader.

The poet indicates what there is to be seen "under the shadow of this red rock" by contrasting it with what will not be seen. It is "something different from either/ Your shadow at morning striding behind you/ Or your shadow at evening rising to meet you," from either memory or desire, from either past or future. It is the eternal present of the human condition: "fear in a handful of dust," for all we are is a handful of dust. The condition of that dust is determined by the spirit which animates it, the spirit which, *The Waste Land* declares, in the present is a decaying, sickened one.

At the heart of that sickness is the culture of romantic love, which makes a cult of love and death, yokes them together, and is essentially barren. The apotheosis of its expression can be found in Richard Wagner's opera, *Tristan und Isolde*, which Eliot evokes by the premonitory four lines beginning "*Frisch weht der Wind*," sung at the beginning of the music drama, as the lovers begin their journey to fatal love and inevitable death. "The fresh wind blows in the direction of home. My Irish girl, do you know," the ominous question is as much directed at the reader now as at Isolde, "where you are heading?"

From the realm of myth and hyper-reality, Eliot segues to the present with a monologue like Marie's. A woman recalls a romantic tryst. "'You gave me hyacinths first a year ago;/ They called me the hyacinth girl.'" There is a tone of dancing innocence in her voice, fitting, as she is identified with a flower, a sort of grace of nature, but something plaintive and desperate is mingled with her liveliness. The flower represents a mythological figure, Hyacinth, who was accidentally killed when the discus thrown by Apollo, the god who loved him, accidentally veered off course, or was deliberately made to do so by Zephyr, the West Wind, who was jealous of their closeness, and killed him. From his blood sprung the flower. In his use of hyacinths, then, Eliot is alluding again to a love mixed with death and to rebirth. In response to "the hyacinth girl" the narrator laments,

> Your arms full, and your hair wet, I could not
> Speak, and my eyes failed, I was neither
> Living nor dead, and I knew nothing,
> Looking into the heart of light, the silence.

He is caught in a twilight state, unable to speak, benumbed, "neither/ Living nor dead," knowing "nothing." "Looking into the heart of light," does not illuminate, just as the sun's blaze earlier only parched. All he experiences from the sensual arousal is silence. Eliot ends the section with a confirmation of despair, reverting to *Tristan* by using the image of a desolate and empty sea, "*Oed' und leer das Meer.*"

III.

The scene shifts to the parlor of a fortune teller who reads tarot cards, Madame Sosostris. In a decaying culture, where people are caught in an abandoned present between a past whose meaning is lost and a future that offers no hope, superstition trumps faith and anxiety accompanies every action. The fortune teller, despite her reputation—"known to be the wisest woman in Europe with a wicked pack of cards"—herself is sick. She has "a bad cold." Whose fortune she is telling, we are not sure—perhaps the poet-narrator's. But she turns up a series of cards, each suggesting aspects of the themes of darkness, decay, and death. There is a drowned Phoenician sailor, a man with three staves, a one-eyed merchant, a mysterious, blank card representing "something he carries on his back,/ Which I am forbidden to see," and, present by its absence, the Hanged Man.

Central to *The Waste Land* is the story of the Fisher King that appears in the medieval romances concerned with the quest for the Holy Grail, a bowl thought to be the vessel from which Jesus drank his last cup of wine and in which Joseph of Arimathea caught the blood dripping from his wounds as he hung upon the cross. Lost thereafter, the bowl became the object of a quest narrated by several medieval authors and undertaken by several knights in the various Grail texts. The quest for the vessel came to symbolize a spiritual quest. In the course of the quest in these narratives, the knights discovered a land under a terrible enchantment, condemned to barrenness. It was ruled over by the Fisher King who was presented as similarly cursed. He was either wounded or sterile, or even

34

dead in his life. And his blighted condition was the cause of his kingdom's blight.

In appropriating this story as an underlying motif for his poem, Eliot also appropriated the interpretation of the story set forth in a study by Jessie L. Weston called *From Ritual to Romance*. Weston argued that the Grail story represented primitive fertility rituals. Through the yearly rite, coordinated with the changing seasons, of killing the king and installing a new king and of mourning a dying god and celebrating a god newly born, people sought to influence their own fertility and the fertility of the land. It is a motif readers will be most familiar with in the legend of King Oedipus of Thebes and in the Christian drama of the crucifixion and the resurrection of Jesus. In *The Waste Land*, Eliot is describing a time after the old king has been killed but before the new one has been born.

Through the symbolic images on the tarot cards, especially the man with three staves and the hanged man, Eliot introduced the dominant image of *The Waste Land*, the wasteland itself. The man with three staves represents the Fisher King himself, Eliot wrote in a series of "Notes on 'The Waste Land,'" attached to the end of the poem, not because of anything inherent in the image but because, Eliot said, he made the association "quite arbitrarily." The hanged man, Eliot noted, is "associated with the Hanged God" whom Sir James Frazer defines in his classic encyclopedia of fertility mythology, *The Golden Bough*, as a fertility god who is sacrificed in order for his resurrection to restore fertility to his land and his people. Thus in the sequence devoted to Madame Sosostris and her tarot pack, Eliot deepens the fundamental problem of the poem. There is a spiritual barrenness in the world. The man with three staves represents the impotent king. The force necessary for fertility, the hanged man, representing the fertility god, is missing. The closing line of the section reflects not just the morbid sensibility of the fortuneteller but the reality of the forsaken world Eliot is presenting: "One must be so careful these days."

Until the conclusion of the first section, the focus of the poem has been on the ruminations of a solitary speaker lost in a decaying, desolate landscape, or it has been on scraps of conversation between people at a loss—in a café, in a room off a garden, at a fortuneteller's. In the final stanza, Eliot presents a garish picture of London as an "Unreal City," where "A crowd of people flowed over London Bridge." The city is peopled by a crowd of living corpses compared, by allusion, to the damned in Dante's hell, "I had not thought death had undone so many." Like the damned "each man" has his eye "fixed … before his feet." There is no hope, nothing to see. Even the church bell when it rings the hour has "a dead sound on the final stroke of nine."

In the crowd, the speaker spots "one I knew" and addresses him. It is a comrade from the war, but "Stetson" was with him "in the ships at Mylae," in the Second Punic War, not on the battlefields of Europe in the First World War, which had ended hardly three years before the actual time of the poem. The battle of Mylae took place in 260 B.C. off the coast of Italy. In that battle, the Romans struck a decisive blow against Carthage. The temporal disorientation confounds the idea that there is material progress through history and reinforces the emptiness of experience that is at the heart of the poem. Moreover, through the conflation of two wars separated by more than twenty centuries, the problem of the barrenness of the land seems to be attributable to an element in people themselves; although time has progressed, human behavior and the human experience remains fixed.

"That corpse," the poet then asks the comrade he has stopped, "you planted last year in your garden,/ Has it begun to sprout? Will it bloom this year?" The joke, comparing a corpse, suggested by either of the wars looming in the background of the poet's consciousness, to a seed, is a bitter one. Yet it is, after all, the miracle of the resurrection that turns a corpse into a seed, whether in Christian or Pagan mythologies. And that is what the poet is waiting for, the end of the blight of barrenness and the return of fertility. But in the apparently nonsensical doggerel, "O keep the Dog far hence, that's friend to men,/ Or with his nails he'll dig it up again!" the obstacle to both the resurrection and to the return of life and fertility is suggested.

The brute within the human—"the dog that's friend to men"—digs up the corpse and insures the continuation of barrenness.

The section ends with Eliot's challenge to the reader to identify with the malaise he is describing when he echoes the final line of the introductory poem to *The Flowers of Evil*, a collection of poems expressing disgust with mankind and the human condition by the nineteenth-century French poet Charles Baudelaire, "You! Hypocritical reader, my double, my brother."

IV.

The second section of *The Waste Land*, "A Game of Chess," opens on a scene of diffuse and frustrated sensuality inside a luxurious but claustrophobic salon. Eliot describes its surface in all its overwhelming sensory richness. A woman sits on a chair that is like a "burnished throne." It "glowed on the marble." A mirror, a "glass," was "held up by standards wrought with fruited vines." A cupid "peeped out" from behind the vines, and "Another hid his eyes behind his wing." The two cupids represent the contrasting attitudes with which the reader can come to the scene, voyeurism and the repression of the desire to look. Shame and ostentation are mixed as are a sensual impulse and a chaste avoidance of the power of sensuality. Flames, reflected in the mirror, rise from a "sevenbranched candelabra." Jewels glitter in satin cases and the scent of perfume spills into the air from "vials of ivory and colored glass."

In this room of stifling opulence was hung a painting of a woodland scene depicting the rape and mutilation of Philomela by Tereus. It is a grim and brutal tale Ovid tells in the sixth book of the *Metamorphoses*.

When the Athenians were attacked by barbarous tribes, Tereus, King of Thrace, came to their aid. In gratitude, Pandion, king of Athens, gave him his daughter Procne in marriage. After a year, she gave birth to their son, Itys. Several years later, Procne told her husband how much she missed her sister, Philomela, how pleased she would be if Tereus would sail to Athens, implore her father to let Phelomela visit her, and bring her sister back to Thrace. Everything was done as she wished, except that when Tereus saw Philomela he was overcome by an overpowering desire for her. In Thrace, before returning to his palace, Tereus took Philomela into the forest, raped her, cut out her tongue to prevent her from telling of what had happened, and imprisoned her in the forest. He told his wife her sister had died at sea and hoped that would be the end of it, but Philomela gave an attendant a cloth into which she had, in symbols, woven the story of her rape and indicated by signs to give it to her sister. Seeing the cloth, Procne understood what had happened.

On the evening of the festival of Bacchus, the god of wine, when women worked themselves into a frenzy, Procne went out into the forest and tore down the gates of Philomela's prison. Together they plotted revenge. Stifling her motherly compassion, Procne slaughtered her son Itys, roasted his flesh and served the dish to his father. When Tereus tasted the dish, he was so delighted, he summoned his son to partake of it, too. Then his wife told him it was Itys he was eating. Enraged he attempted to slay Procne and Philomela, but as they fled his sword they were transformed, Procne into a nightingale, Philomela into a swallow. Tereus became a hawk.

Eliot's description of the room is enclosed in the violent and deadly force of passion. It begins with an allusion to Cleopatra and her barge, for "The Chair she sat in, like a burnished throne,/ Glowed on the marble," echoes Shakespeare's description of Cleopatra sailing on the Nile, where "The barge she sat in, like a burnished throne,/ Burned on the water." It ends with a picture of the rape of Philomela. The idealized romanticism of *Tristan and Isolde* is now brutalized. The illness of passion is shown in the violence of desire and its barrenness in the way it leads to the devouring of progeny.

But that is merely the background. These allusions constitute "withered stumps of time." They are the anterior decorations adorning the present, which is lost in the boredom that oppresses the soul trapped between "memory and desire." The woman in the room is haunted and unnerved by the frustration of everything vital and by the over-stimulating vacuity of the environment. "[H]er hair/ Spread[s] out in fiery points/ Glow[s] into words," but "then would be savagely still." The image representing a woman goes from the voluptuous Cleopatra to the brutalized Philomela to the deadly Medusa with snaky hair, who turned men to stone when they looked at her. When the woman does talk, the rhythm is staccato and she is shown as nervous, insistent, and desperate.

> "My nerves are bad to-night. Yes, bad. Stay with me.
> "Speak to me. Why do you never speak. Speak.
> "What are you thinking of? What thinking? What?
> "I never know what you are thinking. Think."

The voice of her interlocutor is the one which returns in each scene with the same listless despair, a man of weak stone, lost and impotent in his response to every situation. He answers her frenzied questioning with bitter, resignation, "I think we are in rats' alley/ Where the dead men lost their bones." They talk across each other, yet the response of each is oddly appropriate for the utterance of the other. Her frenzy provokes his distance, and his remoteness exacerbates her nervousness. "'What is that noise?'" she asks. "The wind under the door," he answers, as if calming a child's fears. But nothing eases her and she keeps tearing at whatever she can. "'What is that noise now? What is the wind doing?'" And he responds with the same dogged patience one uses when speaking to someone who is unrelentingly demanding and chronically insatiable, "Nothing again nothing." His response nourishes her irritation" "'Do/ You know nothing? Do you see nothing? Do you remember/ Nothing?'" Her question resonates beyond their conversation and suggests both the impotence and disengagement at the heart of the poem—his own comment at line 40 after the scene in the hyacinth garden, "and I knew nothing," and the terrible dialogue between King Lear and his daughter in the first scene of Shakespeare's play, when the repeated use of the word "nothing" becomes the prelude to the death of a king and the decay of social order. His response, "I remember/ Those are pearls that were his eyes," hearkens back to the scene with Madame Sosostris, the tarot reader, who in describing "the drowned Phoenician Sailor," said the very same thing.

The words are Shakespeare's. They come from a song in *The Tempest* that the spirit, Ariel, sings in the mind of Ferdinand, who believes he is the only survivor of a shipwreck in which his father was drowned. Perhaps like the Phoenician sailor? The words suggest, however, not only death but rebirth because Ferdinand's father has not been drowned: The shipwreck in *The Tempest* is illusory. It has been created by the magician Prospero in order to reveal to the voyagers the corrupt condition of their lives and to engineer his own return to life after being cast out of his kingdom and left to die on a barren island. By allusion to *The Tempest*, Eliot makes Shakespeare's play into a metaphor for the condition described in *The Waste Land*. Our lives are depleted and we are on the verge of shipwreck. But we are not really shipwrecked. The barrenness of the world, the impotence of its creatures is an illusory reality. It is caused by an obstruction of vision, which is the result of a passionate attachment to desire.

As if to illustrate the tenacity with which the insufficient world grasps, the woman continues her insistent nagging. And yet the question pains because it pierces. "Are you alive or not?" Inside *The Waste Land*, it is, in fact, difficult to say. Moreover, to illustrate the insufficiency of the world and how little support the culture of the past affords the present, after the woman's second assault, "Is there nothing in your head," the man, who had been reflecting on the cycles of birth and death suggested by *The Tempest*, devalues everything by showing what is in his head—Hamlet's dying cry of "O O O O," followed by a culture-busting, hit song from 1912, called "That Shakespeherian Rag." It begins, "That Shakespeherian rag—/ Most intelligent, very elegant,/ That old classical drag." There seems to be nothing that will sustain, and the woman in her final desperate cry expresses that:

"What shall I do now? What shall I do?
I shall rush out as I am, and walk the street

With my hair down, so. What shall we do tomorrow?
What shall we ever do?"

Her defeated and impotent interlocutor responds with resignation that they will go through the motions of life—"The hot water at ten./ And if it rains, a closed car at four"—awaiting death, the "knock upon the door."

From the boredom and desperation of an elegant salon, Eliot shifts to a dive where he presents a scene in which a cockney woman is telling another woman about her conversation with a third woman whose husband is "coming back" from the war. Unlike just about everything preceding it, the scene is a straightforward melodramatic narrative about the sexual tribulations of a woman who has had five children and an abortion, who is old at thirty-one, and who is still expected to be sexually available and alluring to her husband. It is delivered by an unsympathetic narrator who relates that she told the woman of whom she's gossiping, "if you don't give it him, there's others will," implying herself. The conversation is interrupted several times by the barman's cry "HURRY UP PLEASE IT'S TIME," indicating the bar is closing. The repetition gives the barman's last call a deeper resonance. The story finally is cut short by the closing cry and the section ends with the goodnights of the patrons sliding into the last words Ophelia speaks in *Hamlet* before her death by water, "Good night, ladies, good night, sweet ladies, good night, good night," reinforcing the suggestion of a greater finality than just the end of an evening out at the pub, and once again, also, the inextricability of love and death.

V.

If *The Waste Land* seems to lack coherence because of its fragmentation, approaching it the way one approaches a piece of music may help to give it the structural coherence that makes a work of art aesthetically satisfying. The poem is filled with repetitions, allusions, and quotations, the way a jazz tune is peppered with references to other tunes and to itself, or the

41

way a classical Theme and Variations uses and revises core material to form a complex entity varied in color, emotion, and dynamics but unified by the underlying core material that is variously worked out.

The third section, "The Fire Sermon," for example, after all the desperate turbulence of the previous section, begins, like an elegy, on a note of dark introspection: "The river's tent is broken; the last fingers of leaf/ Clutch and sink into the wet bank. The wind/ Crosses the brown land, unheard. The nymphs are departed." There is an air of tranquility about these lines. They offer a description of a deserted riverbank. In the context of the dry and barren landscape of *The Waste Land*, the riverside, at least, ought to be a fertile area. Yet the nature of its fertility betrays the possibility of renewal. It is a perverse fertility out of which nothing grows but rot.

Eliot transitions from the moody opening lines to a grim description of the river by passing through a quotation from a wedding song by the sixteenth-century English poet Edmund Spenser. The refrain "Sweet Thames run softly till I end my song" taken away from its original text and applied in this new context reflects sharply the contrast between Spenser's fertile, springtime riverscape and Eliot's barren riverside. Spenser's world is alive with nymphs, flowers, bridal couples, and glories all brought together by the poet, despite his own sense of dejection, to celebrate meaningful marriage in a fecund world. In *The Waste Land*, "A rat crept softly through the vegetation/ Dragging its slimy belly on the bank."

The poet sets himself at the river's edge and merges thematically with the impotent Fisher King of the Grail legend, the man with three staves from Madame Sosostris' tarot pack, and Ferdinand from *The Tempest*. He muses "upon the king my brother's wreck/ And the king my father's death before him," and thinks about the death of kings, the disintegration of order that implies, and the consequent loss of meaning in life. From a description of the eternal landscape of decay, the poem slips into the internal mindscape of the poet who imagines death as "White bodies naked on the low damp ground/ And bones cast in the low dry garret/ Rattled by" the sound "of the rat's foot."

The recurring rat embodies the deadly plague destroying the human spirit.

These ruminations give way to a burlesque of Andrew Marvell's poem "To His Coy Mistress," where the pressure of eternity is replaced by the insistent pace of industrial society. "But at my back from time to time I hear," not "Time's winged chariot," as in Marvell's poem, but "The sounds of horns and motor cars." And what this technology brings is not love but love's debasement, "Sweeny to Mrs. Porter in the Spring." Their liaison is celebrated in an allusion to an obscene ditty about a brothel keeper and one of her "girls," which Eliot sanitized: "O the moon shone bright on Mrs. Porter/ And on her daughter/ They wash their feet in soda water." After an ironic juxtaposition of an image of children singing and the reiterated allusion to the plaint of Philomela after her rape and mutilation by Tereus, Eliot offers two illustrations of what he presents as examples of the sexual degeneracy which defines the sterility of the age.

The first scene is set "Under the brown fog of a winter noon" in the "Unreal City" of London, as "Mr. Eugenides" solicits the poet for a weekend sexual rendezvous belying his name and representing the sterility of the age. In "The Burial of the Dead," London was unreal because it was a city of living corpses mechanically pursuing their daily tasks. Now it is unreal in the sense that its inhabitants are out of touch with the fundamental reality of "The ancient pulse of germ and birth," in Thomas Hardy's words. The second instance shows that sterility in a heterosexual encounter. Amid the difficulties and narrative disjunction of The Waste Land, like the scene in the working-class pub, here is a coherent and straightforward narrative.

After a day of mechanical work that turns the human organism into a machine, a "human engine ... Like a taxi throbbing waiting," a typist returns to her flat and prepares dinner. Her underwear is drying on the windowsill, and the divan upon which she sleeps is strewn with other intimate apparel, like her stockings. Eliot evokes a tawdry eroticism in this scene, in contrast to the suffocating suggestion of unsatisfied sensuality he presented in the first part of "A Game of Chess." A young man arrives who is described as "A small house agent's clerk, with one bold stare,/ One of the low on whom assurance sits/ As a silk hat on a Bradford millionaire." His conceit and his appetite, after dinner, do not require that the typist respond to his advances but simply that she does not repulse them. After their alienated sexual exchange, he leaves, "grop[ing] his way, finding the stairs unlit," signifying the condition of moral and vital darkness in which he lives, and she looks in the mirror, adjusts her hair, says to herself she's "glad it's over," and diverts herself by "put[ting] a record on the gramophone." This sexual encounter represents the debasement of the fundamental model of love and fertility. It is neither an act of procreation, nor a ritual performed ceremoniously for a fecund earth, nor even the expression, as in the story of Tristan and Isolde, of turbulent human passion. It is an egotistical assertion of barren self on the clerk's part and an instance of the habitual submission on the typist's. Like the machines they have become, their intercourse is mechanical.

The narrator/poet embeds himself, although only an observer, in this scene, calling himself Tiresias. In the notes he added to the end of the poem, which are often as opaque as the poem they are presumably intended to clarify, Eliot identifies Tiresias as "a mere spectator and not indeed a 'character'… yet the most important personage in the poem, uniting all the rest." Eliot continues, giving a unifying principle to the entire poem, by saying, "Just as the one-eyed merchant, seller of currants, melts into the Phoenician Sailor, and the latter is not wholly distinct from Ferdinand Prince of Naples, so all the women are one woman, and the two sexes meet in Tiresias. What Tiresias *sees*, in fact, is the substance of the poem." Thus the poem represents the narrator's awareness of his anguished relation to history, to culture, to time itself, whether to the crumbled past, the infertile present, or the hopeless future, and to all the human failings he documents. What Tiresias sees in this scene is one of the highest examples of human contact debased into the lowest example of barrenness, selfishness, and alienation.

The figure of Tiresias is a fitting emblem of a point into which all other points converge and merge because of his peculiar fate. The story of Tiresias is told in Book Three of Ovid's *Metamorphoses*. After striking two intertwined snakes he had come upon in the forest, Tiresias changed from a man into a woman. Seven years later, he again came upon those snakes similarly intertwined, and, striking them again changed back from woman to man. When the gods, Jupiter and Juno, were arguing once about who takes more pleasure in the act of love, Juno saying men, Jupiter saying woman, they decided to call upon Tiresias, who had been both sexes, to settle their dispute. To Juno's consternation, he sided with Jupiter. As punishment, Juno blinded him. Although no god is able to undo the work of another, to counter Juno's punishment, Jupiter conferred on Tiresias the ability to know the future. Thus he was a blind seer. Because he is blind, thus powerless, yet able to see the truth, Eliot makes Tiresias the image of the impotent poet trapped in the waste land.

The poet segues from the scene of dismal intercourse between the typist and the clerk back to the barren world of London and into the tormented inner mindscape of his own forlorn consciousness by bleeding the music of the gramophone record into Ariel's music from *The Tempest*, which accompanies Ferdinand's reverie on loss. "This music crept by me upon the waters" and then "along the Strand" and into the city, past the dives and to the grand church of Sir Christopher Wren, St. Magnus Martyr. In the midst of all the decay that edifice, not a ruins, represents an "Ionian splendor," not only in terms of its columns but in terms of the echo of ancient Greece. The historical and architectural coherence of this church endows the church with the suggestion of an inherently consoling and guiding power which nothing else in the poem shares. As yet in Eliot's own life, in 1922, it is only a harbinger of the religious dedication that will culminate in his entrance into the Anglican Church in 1927, which can be seen as his way of freeing himself from the despair of the waste land of the contemporary world.

The third section ends with a shift from narrative descriptions of alienation to a lyrical lament for the modern condition. Derived from the song of the Rhine Maidens in Wagner's *Das Rheingold*, "The river sweats/ Oil and tar" is almost pastoral in its calm depiction of things that fire the furnace of industrial society. It is a background without any human figures. This *tableau vivant* of the river at the beginning of the twentieth century fades into a historical memory. Eliot pictures Queen Elizabeth I and her favorite, the soldier-courtier, and sometimes her political opponent, Robert, Earl of Leicester, sailing on the Thames and flirting. It is an image of frustration. Elizabeth's private affection for Leicester and her role as queen were in conflict. Moreover, she never married and she gave birth to no children.

Eliot ends the section with a tram ride through a dusty landscape to a rendezvous and with sexual debasement, which results in both guilt and indifference: "He wept. He promised a new start.... What should I resent?" That episode leads to an allusion to Saint Augustine's description of being in the grip of unholy sexual passion and surrounded by lust upon his arrival in Carthage and to the Budhha's condemnation of lust through the quotation of the four times repeated word burning in the Budhha's Fire Sermon, an instruction, like Augustine's *Confession*, in asceticism.

VI.

The brief fourth section, "Death by Water," the section that Ezra Pound said was essential when he was editing *The Waste Land*, is a *memento mori*. It is a reminder of death and the fulfillment of Madame Sosostris' warning at the end of the first section when she connected the drowned Phoenician sailor with the poet—"Here, said she/ Is your card"—and with Ferdinand in *The Tempest*, by the allusion to "Those are pearls that were his eyes." Now the Phoenician sailor is dead, and Eliot uses his death to remind us of death: "O you who turn the wheel and look windward,/ Consider Phlebas, who was once handsome and tall as you." To warn those who suffer the death-in-life that Eliot has been portraying may be the one antidote to that condition. Death itself is the agency for bringing forth the recognition of the sacredness of life which may not be wasted in the barren landscape and the meaningless pursuits Eliot has described.

VII.

From the contemplation of human mortality Eliot moves, in the final section, to the death that gives mortality its terror, the death of God. That death renders both human life and human death meaningless. Achieving a sense of finality through the repetition of the word, "After," Eliot recreates the prelude to the crucifixion and its aftermath. "The torchlight red on sweaty faces" suggests the betrayal of Christ when the Roman soldiers come to take him. "The frosty silence," refers to Christ's pain in the garden of Gethsemane. "The agony in stony places" suggests Christ's agony bearing the cross; the "shouting and crying," the pain of the crucifixion then and now. The crucifixion itself represents the mythological slaughter of God that Eliot had referred to earlier. But without a culture meaningfully attuned to the values of the Christian sacrifice, whose customs and ceremonies, to use the words of W. B. Yeats, are corrupt, the ritual of resurrection that concludes the death of god does not occur: "He who was living is now dead/ We who were living are now dying."

As in a piece of music where themes are stated, developed, and then climactically recapitulated, the final section of *The Waste Land* brings back the earlier elements. After the drama of the death of God in the first stanza, Eliot introduces a lament on the loss in the lines beginning, "Here is no water but only rock," recalling line 24 and the parched desert wanderings of the Children of Israel in *Deuteronomy*, when Moses struck a rock and a stream of water flowed from it. But that was in a desert where the spirit of God was present. The waste land is a waste land precisely because of the absence of the Divine spirit. The rock yields no water.

If *The Waste Land* can be thought of as having a plot, it is that God has died and mankind, in consequence, has become barren and the earth is a waste land where nothing can be nourished and grow. At line 360, however, Eliot changes the story and offers a possible hope. With the question, "Who is the third who always walks beside you?" Eliot hints at the answer to his first question, "What are the roots that clutch?" and offers, too, a possible way of thinking about the waste land that offers a way out. In his notes, Eliot wrote that the seven lines beginning with the question on line 360 "were stimulated by" an account of an Antarctic expedition during which "the party of explorers ... had the constant delusion that there was *one more member*" among them than their actual number. A more significant reference, however, is to the final chapter in the Gospel of Luke, particularly to the story of the journey to Emmaus, verses thirteen to thirty-five.

In the first twelve verses, Christ's followers came to the sepulcher after the crucifixion and discovered the rock rolled back and "found not the body of the Lord Jesus." In confirmation of this resurrection, verses thirteen to thirty-five tell the story of two of Jesus' disciples on their way to the town of Emmaus. They encountered a third person who walked beside them on the way. It was Jesus risen, but they did not recognize him. When they arrived in the village, the three sat down together to eat. Jesus broke bread and gave it to them "[a]nd their eyes were opened and they knew him." The last seventeen verses show Jesus resurrected, assuring his disciples of his resurrection.

Within the context of *The Waste Land*, the allusion to the journey to Emmaus signifies 1) that the dying god has, in fact, been reborn and 2) that his apparent absence—the cause of the barrenness of the waste land—is *not* the god's actual absence but mankind's inability to recognize him even when he is present.

This insight can be transformative, for it suggests there must be a way to develop the ability to see the divine. It leads in the next verse paragraph, beginning "What is that sound high in the air," to overt lamentation. The "Murmur of maternal lamentation" indicates a shift of attention away from the impotent and half-dead father to the mother alive with grief. In the next line, because of their proximity to the image of the grieving Mary, "the hooded hordes swarming/ Over endless plains, stumbling in cracked earth/ Ringed by the flat horizon only" become objects of pity. They are no longer the images of alienation that the crowds swarming over London Bridge had been at the end of the first section. And then the violent history of western civilization is encapsulated in the image of ruined cities as they are catalogued, "Falling towers/ Jerusalem Athens Alexandria/ Vienna London." All of them are "Unreal." The retreat from the violence of history and the barrenness of the present is contained in the word "Unreal." The things that are and that are unsatisfactory are "unreal." Reality exists on another plane of perception. The plane of perception that appears to the senses is a disturbed one which Eliot shows in its phantasmagorical madness in the stanza beginning "A woman drew her long black hair out tight/ And fiddled whisper music on those strings." This image and the ones that follow show humanity mesmerized by demonic powers, like the Medusa, and transformed into blood-sucking monsters, like the "bats with baby faces," through a destabilizing sensuality.

Confronting the horror, not just the barrenness of modern life, breaks the dry spell. A cock crows in line 393, representing the prelude to the crucifixion and the betrayal of Christ by Peter, whom Jesus foretold would betray him three times before the cock crowed. The line signifies not only the denial of God but the dawn of a new consciousness that may break the barren spell and restore fertility: "In a flash of lightning. Then a damp gust/ Bringing rain." The landscape has changed from the desert waste land of Western Europe to the jungle of India, where the holy river, Ganges, is low and "black clouds/ Gathered … over" one of the Himalayan mountains. The scriptural focus has also changed from Christian to Hindu as Eliot alludes to a fable from the Hindu holy scriptures, the Upanishads.

In this story, gods, men, and demons ask Prajapati, the Creator, to teach them what is necessary to know. He repeats the syllable, "DA" to each. It is, like *The Waste Land* itself, a fragment open to interpretation. The gods interpret it to stand for the word, "Datta," give alms; men, "Dayadhvam," have compassion; demons, "Damyata," practice self-control. Each injunction becomes a defining theme which Eliot explores in a series of images. The essential nature of giving is surrender, "The awful daring of a moment's surrender/ Which an age of prudence can never retract/ By this, and this only, we have existed." The text is ambiguous. Is the moment's surrender a surrender of divine imprudence, which gives the self to the eternal? Or is it the imprudent surrender to desire, which locks one in this illusory world?

For compassion, Eliot imagines "each in his prison," after his own particular key has turned and locked him into his own self-defined imprisonment. Imprisonment signifies coming upon the person one really is and whom one has desperately attempted to avoid confronting. To represent such a person in such a condition, Eliot alludes to Shakespeare's Coriolanus, the overly proud Roman military hero who turned against Rome; he was humbled in his pride and overcome by his enemy. The despair that has been the on-going response throughout the poem to the misguided living dead is replaced by compassion. For self-control, Eliot uses the image of a boat responding "Gaily, to the hand expert with sail and oar." To that he compares a heart longing to respond, "beating obedient/ To controlling hands." Only through disciplined obedience to a controlling force, the poet assets, can the demonic powers that shipwreck us be stilled.

Before the concluding verse paragraph, Eliot has achieved knowledge of what is necessary for salvation, for extricating himself from the waste land. It is the discipline implicit in the three DAs and the act of putting himself in "controlling hands" which can command a heart and make it beat obediently. But knowledge of what is needed is not the same as attaining what is necessary. And the last stanza of the poem, a rondo of allusions, is a lament and a prayer rather than a crossing over into a new land. Additionally, the focus is more on the poet himself, rather than on his milieu. This suggests that the entire poem may be understood as a depiction of the poet's own troubled soul constructed from the fragments of images gathered from the world around him. The poem, then, as Eliot suggested, really is an anatomy of "Tiresias," that is, of the poet, but through indirection. It is as if a painter were to paint a self-portrait not by painting his face but by painting what his face sees, by identifying himself through the identification of what surrounds him.

"I sat upon the shore," Eliot writes, focusing on himself, "Fishing, with the arid plain behind me." "Behind me" suggests both geographical and spiritual position. The arid plain is behind him the way one might say an unhappy event is "behind me," after it is finished. "Shall I at least set my lands in order?" he asks then, as if he were making preparation for death. Death, according to the dominant myth of *The Waste Land*, is the precondition for life: the god dies so that the god can be reborn; the seasons of the earth's fertility turn: the earth dies so that it can be reborn and produce a new harvest. Thus the final images that swirl through the last lines of the poem suggest destruction prior to reconstitution. The nursery rhyme, "London Bridge is falling down falling down falling down," appears, recalling the crowd of the living dead who "flowed over London Bridge" at line 62. At the end of the poem, there is a vision of the destruction. The apocalyptic nature of that destruction is reinforced by the next line, from Dante's *Purgatory*, "Then he dived back into the fire that refines them." Purgation of sin through a refiner's fire is a precondition for emerging from the condition of death-in-life that Eliot has been describing. It becomes clear, too, that the condition of death-in-life is the state of sin.

In the next line, "When shall I be as the swallow," Eliot recalls the central sin of *The Waste Land*, the rape and mutilation of Philomela by Tereus, the speaker longing for his own metamorphosis, like Philomela's transformation into a swallow. His final depiction of himself is as a prince whose tower is ruined. He is an impotent man, like the Fisher King. But the poet has collected the fragments which constitute the poem in an effort to support his ruins: what is left to him will not crumble entirely. But as *The Waste Land* ends, alluding to Thomas Kyd's *The Spanish Tragedy*, the poet senses the return of madness, that he has not transcended his condition or his era. He repeats the instruction for salvation of Prajapati, give

alms, be compassionate, be controlled, and ends three times
repeating the Hindu word "Shantih," which Eliot states in his
notes signifies "the peace which passeth understanding." He
uses this word as a sort of prayer, a *dona nobis pacem*, uttered
from the depth of his despair, rather than as a description of a
condition he has attained.

Critical Views

ELEANOR COOK ON MAPS OF *THE WASTE LAND*

The Waste Land requires three maps for its place-names. One is a map of Greater London and the lower Thames, for the poem is a London poem even in its final form. One early plan, as Hugh Kenner has argued,[1] conceived of Part III as a vision of London through various Augustan modes, making of the city almost another character, and suggesting a geographical unity as focal point for the poem. At this stage, says Kenner, "the rest of the poem seems to have been planned around it [Part III], guided by the norms and decorums of an Augustan view of history" (p. 35). Then Eliot wrote Part V, the vision of an urban apocalypse became dominant, and Part III was cut accordingly.

The Waste Land is not only a London poem; it is also a European poem, or more precisely a Mediterranean poem. It was always so through the early drafts, and it became noticeably so when, in Part V, London was listed as the last in a series of five great cities, Jerusalem, Athens, Alexandria, Vienna, London. The poem therefore requires a second map for those place-names that are not from the London area, leaving aside the names of Ganga and the Himavant. If those place-names are plotted on a map, they may be seen to ring the Mediterranean in the following sense. The northerly names are not seen as centers, in the way our twentieth-century eyes see them. Rather, they balance Carthage and Mylae to the south, and Jerusalem and Smyrna (now Izmir) to the east. This map coincides roughly with the Roman Empire at its most expansive, and therefore also coincides roughly with the theater of war during World War I. The center of this second map is Rome.

This leaves us with the names of Ganga and the Himavant. The map that is useful here is a very simple and a very symmetrical one: it is Dante's map of the inhabited world.[2] The exact center of this world is Jerusalem. Ninety degrees to the east is the eastern limit, the mouths of the Ganges, which is also the eastern limit of *The Waste Land*. Ninety degrees to the west is the western limit, Gibraltar or the western end of the Mediterranean, which is also the western limit of *The Waste Land*. Precisely halfway between Gibraltar and Jerusalem is Rome. We have thus three maps, one of a city, one of an empire, one of a world. They are not set side by side; that is, we do not make orderly progression from one map to the next in the poem. Rather, it is as if they were layered, and we read meaning from one map into another. Urban vision, imperial vision, world vision: each illuminates the other.

The English Augustans, Mr. Kenner observes, saw encouraging parallels between their London and Rome at the time of Augustus. Eliot's early plan for *The Waste Land*, mentioned above, was to develop satiric parallels between modern London and Augustan London. Mr. Kenner argues persuasively that Eliot "may well have had in mind at one time a kind of modern *Aeneid*, the hero crossing seas to pursue his destiny, detained by one woman and prophesied to by another, and encountering visions of the past and the future, all culminated in a city both founded and yet to be founded, unreal and oppressively real, the Rome through whose past Dryden saw London's future" (pp. 39–40). London was to be "the original Fisher King as well as the original Waste Land, resembling Augustine's Carthage as Dryden's London had resembled Ovid's Rome" (p. 28). With the final revisions, however, the center of the poem became "the urban apocalypse, the great City dissolved into a desert ..." (p. 46).

But I wonder whether the pre-eminent pattern for London from first to last was not Rome. Of course, in one sense all the cities in the final version of *The Waste Land* are the same: they are Cities of Destruction. But the poem nonetheless focuses on one particular city, London. Similarly, I think that the poem focuses on one prototype for London, and that the prototype is Rome, the center of the second map, and the center of the western half of the third map. Among these three maps, studies of *The Waste Land* have tended to concentrate on the first and the third, Eliot's urban vision and his world vision. But London in 1922 was still the center of an empire. What I want to concentrate on here is Eliot's vision of imperial apocalypse in *The Waste Land*, working from the hypothesis that a vision of Rome and the Roman Empire lies behind Eliot's vision of London and the British Empire.

Rome could provide a pattern for London in *The Waste Land* for good reason. The most obvious is that Rome was once both a great city and the capital of a great empire. In this, she is no different from those other great cities in Part V that were also capitals of great though very different empires: "Jerusalem, Athens, Alexandria, / Vienna, London." This list is worth examining. Eliot preserves the chronological order of the flourishing of each empire. He lists three ancient empires in one line, two modern ones in the following line. The large gap between the three ancient and two modern empires is dominated by Rome, who—and here she differs from the other cities—held sway over all three old empires. The name of Vienna, capital of the Austro-Hungarian Empire, suggests a line of succession, for the Austro-Hungarian Empire saw itself as heir to the Holy Roman Empire, which in turn saw itself as heir to the Roman Empire. Eliot was explicit about part of this line of succession in 1951:

> For Virgil's conscious mind, it [destiny] means the imperium romanum.... I think that he had few illusions and that he saw clearly both sides of every question—the case for the loser as well as the case for the winner.... And do you really think that Virgil was mistaken? You must remember that the Roman Empire was transformed into the Holy Roman Empire. What Virgil proposed to his contemporaries was the highest ideal even for an unholy Roman Empire, for any merely temporal empire. We are all, so far as we inherit the civilization of Europe, still citizens of the Roman Empire.... It remains an ideal, but one which Virgil passed on to Christianity to develop and to cherish.[3]

This is the older Eliot speaking. The younger Eliot was quite detached about Christianity, but Eliot always saw himself as heir to the riches of classical civilization, and especially Roman civilization. "Tradition and the Individual Talent" appeared in 1919, and in 1923 Eliot wrote in the *Criterion*: "If everything derived from Rome were withdrawn—everything we have from Norman-French society, from the Church, from Humanism, from every channel direct and indirect, what would be left? A few Teutonic roots and husks. England is a 'Latin' country ..." (*Criterion*, 2 [October 1923], 104).

"For at least seven years, it would seem," writes Kenner, "an urban apocalypse had haunted Eliot's imagination" (p. 42). To an imagination thus haunted, and brooding from 1919 onward[4] over material for what was to be *The Waste Land*, it might very well have appeared that the inheritance of Rome was disintegrating. "I am all for empires," wrote Eliot in January of 1924, "especially the Austro-Hungarian Empire."[5] But the Austro-Hungarian Empire had just been broken up by the Treaty of Versailles in 1919. And Christianity, considered simply as a force in history in the way Henry Adams saw it, might also be disintegrating. "The struggle of 'liberal' against 'orthodox' faith is out of date," Eliot wrote as early as 1916. "The present conflict is far more momentous than that."[6] The ghost of Rome prevails in *The Waste Land* because Rome evolved from the greatest of Western empires into a Christian one; because the various European empires that followed Rome, all the way down to the British Empire, retained something of this inheritance, including the association of church and state (at least, officially); and because Eliot at the time of *The Waste Land* sees the possibility that this inheritance and this association will come to an end in the disintegration of church and state and civilization as we know them. "Eliot ... once said to me," Spender recalls, "that *The Waste Land* could not have been written at any moment except when it was written—a remark which, while biographically true in regard to his own life, is also true of the poem's time in European history after World War I. The sense that Western civilization was in a state which was the realization of historic doom lasted from 1920 to 1926."[7]

Notes

1. "The Urban Apocalypse," in A. Walton Litz, ed., *Eliot in His Time: Essays on the Occasion of the Fiftieth Anniversary of The Waste Land* (Princeton, 1973), pp. 23–49.
2. *The Divine Comedy* (Temple Classics edition), *Paradiso*, canto xxvii, n. 11.
3. "Virgil and the Christian World," broadcast from London, Sept. 9, 1951; reprinted in *T. S. Eliot: Selected Prose*, ed. John Hayward (London, 1953), p. 97.
4. And perhaps earlier. "I hope to get started on a poem I have in mind" (Eliot to John Quinn, Nov. 5, 1919); he hopes "to write a long poem I have had on my mind for a long time" (Eliot to his mother, Dec. 18, 1919); in *The Waste Land: A Facsimile and Transcript of the Original Drafts including the Annotations of Ezra Pound*, ed. Valerie Eliot (New York 1971), xviii.
5. *Transatlantic Review*, 1 (January 1924), 95.
6. *International Journal of Ethics*, 27 (1916), 117.
7. Stephen Spender, *T. S. Eliot* (New York, 1975), pp. 117–18.

LOUIS MENAND ON NINETEENTH CENTURY STYLE

The composition of *The Waste Land* was a famously difficult business. The story of Eliot's troubles is now well enough known to have become, for many readers, part of the experience of the poem.[1] Having been shoring fragments for a long work since his first year in England, Eliot announced his intention to begin putting his poem together in the fall of 1919, but apparently found it almost impossible to proceed. "[E]very evening, he went home to his flat hoping that he could start writing again, and with every confidence that the material was *there* and waiting," he told Conrad Aiken, but "night after night the hope proved illusory: the sharpened pencil lay unused by the untouched sheet of paper. What could be the matter? He didn't know."[2] His writer's block was aggravated by circumstances: the demands of his job at Lloyds Bank, and of the various freelance lecturing assignments he took on to supplement his salary, left him with little energy for poetry; his wife's father became ill, then his wife, then Eliot himself; and a visit from his mother and sister in the summer of 1921 seems to have precipitated a crisis. He took three months' leave from the bank in October 1921, and went first to Margate for a month, then to Lausanne to undergo therapy; and there, working in solitude, he was able to complete a draft of the poem. Pound performed his editorial role in January, and *The Waste Land* seems finally to have been finished in the late spring or early summer of 1922.

Eliot alludes often in his letters during this period to personal troubles—to concern about the state of his marriage, anxiety about his career, recurrent nervous exhaustion, even the fear of mental illness—and it may be, as Ronald Bush has suggested, that the combined traumatic weight of these worries made writing poetry under ordinary conditions impossible by compelling Eliot to confront emotional material that a commitment to literary honesty made nearly intractable.[3] And there seems to have been a purely professional pressure on Eliot as well, the pressure caused by the regular appearance on his desk at *The Egoist* of the chapters of *Ulysses* in manuscript from, which made him feel about his own work, as he explained it to an interviewer many years later, that "[w]hat he was tentatively attempting to do, with the usual false starts and despairs, had already been done, done superbly and, it seemed to him finally, in prose which without being poetic in the older sense, had the intensity and texture of poetry."[4]

But *The Waste Land* must have been difficult to write for another, simpler reason. It was the promised major work of a writer who, in his criticism, had exposed the delusiveness of virtually every conventional prescription for poetical newness. In a period when avant-garde literature seemed a function of theories and manifestos, Eliot was an avant-gardist without a program. Having demonstrated the factitiousness of the traditional building blocks of poetic theory—the definition of what literature is, the epistemological explanation of how literature works, the notion that sincerity is a matter of being true to oneself—Eliot must have found himself with nothing to construct a poem on. Whatever their insight into the way literature is perceived, his prescriptive essays are, from a writer's point of view, entirely impractical: the fourth of the

"Reflections on Contemporary Poetry" describes genuine creativity as a business as unpremeditated as falling in love, and "Tradition and the Individual Talent" assigns the poet the whole of the Western tradition as homework but says nothing about how that learning might, in the actual process of composition, be put to use.

"[I]f we are to express ourselves, our variety of thoughts and feelings, on a variety of subjects with inevitable rightness," one of the early essays counsels the modern poet, "we must adapt our manner to the moment with infinite variations."[5] The sentence might have been the model for many of Eliot's early critical prescriptions. It is a formula whose lack of metaphysical content may be satisfying to the skeptic, but whose lack of almost every other sort of content leaves the practitioner somewhat worse off than he was without the advice, for it provokes the question, What is one's manner if it is a thing infinitely adaptable? But let us suppose that this was a question that Eliot, as he sat, a poem in his mind but a blank sheet before him, asked himself at some point. It would not have seemed unfamiliar to him, for it is a particular instance of the general question posed by the extreme ontological relativism of his dissertation: if each thing is entirely a function of its perceived relation to every other thing, what sense does it make for us to speak—as we do speak—of an object's distinctive character? Individuality—the set of qualities that "belong" to the object—is, by the lights of the dissertation, a phantom; it is an accident of the shape ordinary knowledge happens to take, the inexplicable residue that remains after everything else about a thing has been explained, or the unlikeness that is left after all likenesses have been used up. The notion that there are qualities original to the object persists because we have made the decision to treat certain aspects of our experience as discrete. But philosophically these discriminations have no standing; they cannot survive analysis, whose virtue, the dissertation reminds us, "is in showing the destructibility of everything."[6]

This might seem a problem whose working out will be of interest only to metaphysicians and their antagonists; but it is one of those apparently empty philosophical topics that take on life in controversies in which the issues seem quite tangible and the consequences are real enough. The question that Eliot might, in some form or other, have asked himself—What is "mine" about my poem?—is a version of this problem, and it belongs to an important line of nineteenth-century thought. The line is important because it was one of the ways the nineteenth century undertook to defend the status of human endeavor against the implications of scientific determinism, and its consequences mattered because the way the question is answered has an effect on the value that is attributed to art. There is much in Eliot's early writing that can be explained by this nineteenth-century intellectual background; but it is, characteristically, hard to know which side of the issue Eliot wanted to come down on. For if "Tradition and the Individual Talent" seems to lean toward one sort of answer to the question, *The Waste Land* seems to lean in a rather different direction. As is the case with many of the issues that figure in modernist writing, the alternative ways of thinking about the problem can be found articulated in particularly vivid forms in the literature of the 1890s.

(...)

Sitting at his desk with a blank sheet before him, Eliot must thus have felt that in order to write a poem about the experience of contemporary life, he would have to write a poem that took in everything. And *The Waste Land* is indeed a literary work that seems to regard the present moment—as it is experienced by the individual subject—as a reinscription of the whole of the cultural past, and the cultural past as though it were the autobiography of a single consciousness. Or so, at least, the notes to the poem suggest. "Tiresias," explains the note to line 218,

> although a mere spectator and not indeed a "character," is yet the most important personage in the poem, uniting all the rest. Just as the one-eyed merchant, seller of currants,

melts into the Phoenician Sailor, and the latter is not wholly distinct from Ferdinand Prince of Naples, so all the women are one woman, and the two sexes meet in Tiresias. What Tiresias *sees*, in fact, is the substance of the poem.[16]

And the "one woman" of which all the women in the poem are said to be types seems very like a version of Pater's emblem for the evolutionary history of consciousness summed up in the expression of a single face, La Gioconda. Eliot's symbol of perpetual life appears first in the epigraph as the ancient Sybil who cannot die, and again, perhaps, in "The Burial of the Dead" as "Belladonna, the Lady of the Rocks" ("She is older than the rocks among which she sits ..." runs Pater's description).[17] She is the woman in "The Game of Chess," surrounded by "her strange synthetic perfumes" and on whose dressing-room walls hang the "withered stumps of time"—the artistic record of the mythical past ("... and all this has been to her but as the sound of lyres and flutes, and lives only in the delicacy with which it has moulded the changing lineaments, and tinged the eyelids and the hands"). And she appears, finally, in "The Fire Sermon," where she draws "her long black hair out tight," while

> bats with baby faces in the violet light
> Whistled, and beat their wings
> And crawled head downward down a blackened wall

("... like the vampire, she has been dead many times, and learned the secrets of the grave").[18]

But *The Waste Land* makes a strange gloss on "Tradition and the Individual Talent," for it seems infected with a doubt not addressed by the essay, but implicit in the intellectual tradition to which the essay belongs. The doubt stems from the assault the historicist thesis, in the name of subjectivity, makes on the integrity of the individual subject: for after everything in the poem that belongs to the tradition has been subtracted, what sort of value can be claimed for what is left?

Pater called the remainder "style," and he made it the signal—in fact, the single—virtue of the literary object; but in Eliot's essay, all the emphasis is directed the other way. The writer who, in obedience to "Tradition and the Individual Talent"'s "programme for the *métier* of poetry,"[19] undertakes to produce the "really new" work of art, is given no place to look for its origins; the program is distinctly inhospitable to such notions as the Paterian "inner vision." And the suspicion thus arises that newness is nothing more than a kind of accident, a mistake that could not, in the end, be avoided. The manner in which *The Waste Land* dramatizes this doubt derives from the critique of the historicist defense of culture, a critique to which Eliot himself, in his brief career as a philosopher, made a relevant contribution.

(...)

All the difficulties with the late-nineteenth-century idea of style seem to be summed up in *The Waste Land*. It is, to begin with, a poem that includes an interpretation—and one "probably not in accordance with the facts of its origin"—as part of *the poem*, and it is therefore a poem that makes a problem of its meaning precisely by virtue of its apparent (and apparently inadequate) effort to explain itself. We cannot understand the poem without knowing what it meant to its author, but we must also assume that what the poem meant to its author will not be its meaning. The notes to *The Waste Land* are, by the logic of Eliot's philosophical critique of interpretation, simply another riddle—and not a separate one—to be solved. They are, we might say, the poem's way of treating itself as a reflex, a "something not intended as a sign," a gesture whose full significance it is impossible, by virtue of the nature of gestures, for the gesturer to explain.[38]

And the structure of the poem—a text followed by an explanation—is a reproduction of a pattern that, as the notes themselves emphasize, is repeated in miniature many times inside the poem itself, where cultural expressions are transformed, by the mechanics of allusion, into cultural gestures. For each time a literary phrase or a cultural motif is transposed into a new context—and the borrowed motifs in *The Waste Land* are shown to have themselves been borrowed by a succession of cultures[39]—it is reinterpreted, its previous meaning becoming incorporated by distortion into a new meaning suitable to a new use. So that the work of Frazer and Weston is relevant both because it presents the history of religion as a series of appropriations and reinscriptions of cultural motifs, and because it is itself an unreliable reinterpretation of the phenomena it attempts to describe. The poem (as A. Walton Litz argued some time ago) is, in other words, not about spiritual dryness so much as it is about the ways in which spiritual dryness has been *perceived*.[40] And the relation of the notes to the poem proper seems further emblematic of the relation of the work as a whole to the cultural tradition it is a commentary on. *The Waste Land* is presented as a contemporary reading of the Western tradition, which (unlike the "ideal order" of "Tradition and the Individual Talent") is treated as a sequence of gestures whose original meaning is unknown, but which every new text that is added to it makes a bad guess at.

The author of the notes seems to class himself with the cultural anthropologists whose work he cites. He reads the poem as a coherent expression of the spiritual condition of the social group in which it was produced. But the author of the *poem*, we might say, does not enjoy this luxury of detachment. He seems, in fact, determined to confound, even at the cost of his own sense of coherence, the kind of interpretive knowingness displayed by the author of the notes. The author of the poem classes himself with the diseased characters of his own work—the clairvoyante with a cold, the woman whose nerves are bad, the king whose insanity may or may not be feigned. He cannot distinguish what he intends to reveal about himself from what he cannot help revealing: he would like to believe that his poem is expressive of some general reality, but he fears that it is only the symptom of a private disorder. For when he looks to the culture around him, everything appears only as a reflection of his own breakdown: characters and objects metamorphose up and down the evolutionary scale; races and religions lose their purity ("Bin gar keine Russin, stamm' aus Litauen, echt deutsch"); an adulterated "To His Coy Mistress" describes the tryst between Sweeney and Mrs. Porter, and a fragmented *Tempest* frames the liaison of the typist and the young man carbuncular; "London bridge is falling down." The poem itself, as a literary object, seems an imitation of this vision of degeneration: nothing in it can be said to point to the poet, since none of its stylistic features is continuous, and it has no phrases or images that cannot be suspected of—where they are not in fact identified as—belonging to someone else. *The Waste Land* appears to be a poem designed to make trouble for the conceptual mechanics not just of ordinary reading (for what poem does not try to disrupt those mechanics?) but of *literary* reading. For insofar as reading a piece of writing as literature is understood to mean reading it for its style, Eliot's poem eludes a literary grasp.

But the composition of *The Waste Land* was not a reflex, of course, and Eliot was not trying to produce a text determined entirely by submission to outer circumstance and inner compulsion; he was trying, I think, to write a poem that would be "his own." And for such an intention, "style," as the late nineteenth century conceived it, would have restricted what was his in his poem precisely by drawing a line between what could and could not be helped. For, as we have seen, in preserving something in the work of art the artist can truly call his own, Wilde and Pater handed over nearly everything to external forces—to the given. But by renouncing as an illusion the very value aestheticism had rescued from the flux, Eliot's poem seems to have won an even greater authority. For it was the common argument of *The Waste Land*'s early champions— Wilson (1922), Richards (1925), Leavis (1932)—that the poem was held together not by its meaning, or by its author's beliefs, or by metaphysics, but by the unity of a single, coherent authorial presence.[41] If we want to account for this perception of a work that appears so radically decentered—and to do so by saying something more specific to the case than that *The Waste Land* is a poem that takes advantage of the universal habit of reading by which we infer an author for every text—we might suggest that insofar as style had become a problematic literary value, *The Waste Land* was a poem that succeeded by presenting itself as a symptom. For the result of this strategy is that since nothing in *The Waste Land* (except the notes, of course, whose self-consciously "authorial" manner only makes the symptomatic character of the rest appear more striking) is more "Eliot's" than anything else, everything in *The Waste Land* is Eliot's. Eliot appears nowhere, but his fingerprints are on everything. And this gives him a victory over hermeneutics as well, for there is no level of reading of Eliot's poem at which it is possible to say that we have reached a meaning that might not have been put there by Eliot himself.

This view of *The Waste Land* belongs to the school that takes the poem to be a work of "decreation," as Frank Kermode has called it, or a "roadway to nowhere," in Eloise Knapp Hay's more recent phrase;[42] it differs from the school that takes the poem to be a signpost pointing toward "a further stage in [Eliot's] development," or an account of "the trials of a life in the process of becoming exemplary."[43] If the poem was indeed intended as a kind of deliberate dead end, an explosion of the nineteenth-century metaphysics of style leaving nothing in its place, this ambition was perhaps one of the things Eliot learned from Joyce. *Ulysses*, Eliot told Virginia Woolf in a famous conversation, "destroyed the whole of the 19th century. It left Joyce with nothing to write another book on. It showed up the futility of all the English styles.... [T]here was no 'great conception': that was not Joyce's intention.... Joyce did completely what he meant to do."[44] An essay Eliot published in the *Nouvelle Revue Française* a few months after this conversation gives us a better idea of the nature of the accomplishment he had in mind: "The influence of [the style of] Walter Pater," he says there,

... culminates and disappears, I believe, in the work of James Joyce.... In *Ulysses* this influence, like the influence of Ibsen and every other influence to which Mr. Joyce has submitted, is reduced to zero. It is my opinion that

Ulysses is not so distinctly a precursor of a new epoch as it is a gigantic culmination of an old. In this book Joyce has arrived at a very singular and perhaps unique literary distinction: the distinction of having, not in a negative but a very positive sense, no style at all. I mean that every sentence Mr. Joyce writes is peculiarly and absolutely his own; that his work is not a pastiche; but that nevertheless, it has none of the marks by which a "style" may be distinguished.

Mr. Joyce's work puts an end to the tradition of Walter Pater, as it puts an end to a great many other things....[45]

We are likely to feel that traditions are not so easily killed off as the modernists supposed, that they live on long after their metaphysics have been demolished. But this strange life of the buried past is one of the things *The Waste Land*—and its tradition—are all about.

Notes

1. The fullest biographical account of the writing of *The Waste Land* is the one provided by Valerie Eliot in the introduction to her edition of *The Waste Land: A Facsimile and Transcript of the Original Drafts* (New York: Harcourt Brace Jovanovich, 1971), pp. ix–xxix. Lyndall Gordon provides a detailed study of the evolution of the manuscript in *Eliot's Early Years* (Oxford: Oxford University Press, 1977), pp. 86–109, 143–46.

2. Conrad Aiken, "An Anatomy of Melancholy," in *T. S. Eliot: The Man and His Work*, ed. Allen Tate (New York: Dell, 1966), p. 195.

3. See Ronald Bush, *T. S. Eliot: A Study in Character and Style* (New York: Oxford University Press, 1984), pp. 67–72.

4. Anthony Cronin, "A Conversation with T. S. Eliot About the Connection Between *Ulysses* and *The Waste Land*," *The Irish Times*, 16 June 1971, p. 10. The conversation took place in the late 1950s.

5. "Whether Rostand Had Something About Him," *The Athenaeum*, 25 July 1919, p. 665. Eliot was commenting on his sense that the effort to avoid rhetoric had become a rhetoric itself.

6. *Knowledge and Experience in the Philosophy of F. H. Bradley* (London: Faber and Faber, 1964), p. 157. Eliot's dissertation is discussed herein in chapter two.

16. Quotations from *The Waste Land* are from the Boni and Liveright edition (1922), reprinted at the end of *The Waste Land: A Facsimile and Transcript of the Original Drafts*, ed. Valerie Eliot.

17. Grover Smith makes this identification in "T. S. Eliot's Lady of the Rocks," *Notes and Queries*, 194 (19 March 1949), 123–25. "The Madonna of the Rocks" is the title given to another Leonardo portrait.

18. Pater, p. 99. Crawling down a wall head first is a habit of vampires, one exhibited by the hero of Bram Stoker's popular *Dracula* (1897). In an earlier version of this passage in *The Waste Land*, the woman gives way first to a vampire, then to a man who wishes not to be reborn, and finally to something like the "diver in deep seas" of Pater's description (see *The Waste Land* facsimile, pp. 113–15).

19. *The Sacred Wood*, p. 52.

38. It is part of the tradition of *Waste Land* hermeneutics to regard the notes as more or less incidental to the poem proper, and therefore as bits of text that can be treated selectively—some notes may be considered more applicable than others, at the discretion of the commentator—and at face value, as meaning what they say in a way the rest of the poem is assumed not to. (Thus, for instance, the poem has been reprinted in various anthologies, including *The Norton Anthology of English Literature*, with editorial annotations of some lines interspersed among Eliot's own notes.) It is true, of course, that *The Waste Land* was first published without the notes, which Eliot added for the book edition; but they appeared together in every subsequent reprinting. The relevance of Eliot's graduate paper on interpretation alone, not to mention the larger intellectual background I have sketched in, seems enough to justify an approach that considers the notes as part of the poem; but even if Eliot did intend the notes to be straightforward elucidations of the meaning, or some part of the meaning, of his poem, on what hermeneutical grounds can they be considered differently from the rest of the text?

It might be noted that when Arnold Bennett asked Eliot, in 1924, whether the notes to *The Waste Land* were "a skit," Eliot answered that "they were serious, and not more of a skit than some things in the poem itself" (*The Journals of Arnold Bennett*, ed. Newman Flower [London: Cassell, 1933], III, 52; entry for 10 September 1924). For Eliot's own comments on the circumstances of publication that led to the production of the notes, see "The Frontiers of Criticism" (1956), in *On Poetry and Poets* (New York: Farrar, Straus and Cudahy, 1957), pp. 121–22. It is natural (on my view of the poem) that Eliot should generally have disparaged the explanatory (as opposed to the literary) significance of the notes—they are, in any case, fairly self-disparaging as they stand—since their interpretive inadequacy is precisely their point.

39. The conflation, for instance, of the iconography of the Tarot pack, the symbolic figures of Frazer's vegetation rites, and the mythology of Christianity (highlighted by the note to line 46).

40. See A. Walton Litz, *"The Waste Land* Fifty Years After," in *Eliot in His Time*, ed. Litz (Princeton: Princeton University Press, 1973), p. 7.

41. See Edmund Wilson, Jr., "The Poetry of Drouth," *The Dial*, 73 (December 1922), 611–16 ("the very images and the sound of the words—even when we do not know precisely why he has chosen them—are charged with a strange poignancy which seems to bring us into the heart of the singer" [p. 616]); I. A. Richards, *Principles of Literary Criticism*, 2d ed. (1925; rpt. New York and London: Harcourt Brace Jovanovich, n.d.), pp. 289–95 ("the poem still remains to be read.... But that is not difficult to those who still know how to give their feelings precedence to their thoughts, who can accept and unify an experience without trying to catch it in an intellectual net or to squeeze out a doctrine.... The ideas [in Eliot's poetry] ... combine into a coherent whole of feeling and attitude" [pp. 292–3]); F. R. Leavis, *New Bearings in English Poetry* (London: Chatto and Windus, 1932), pp. 90–113 ("the unity of *The Waste Land* is no more 'metaphysical' than it is narrative or dramatic.... The unity the poem aims at is that of an inclusive consciousness" [p. 103]).

42. See Frank Kermode, "A Babylonish Dialect," in *T. S. Eliot: The Man and His Work*, ed. Tate, p. 240; and Eloise Knapp Hay, *T. S. Eliot's Negative Way* (Cambridge, Mass., and London: Harvard University Press, 1982), p. 48.

43. See A. D. Moody, *Thomas Stearns Eliot: Poet* (Cambridge: Cambridge University Press, 1979), p. 79; and Gordon, *Eliot's Early Years*, p. 110.

44. Virginia Woolf, *The Diary of Virginia Woolf*, ed. Anne Olivier Bell, II (New York and London: Harcourt Brace Jovanovich, 1978), 203. Entry for 26 September 1922.

45. "Contemporary English Prose," *Vanity Fair*, 20 (July 1923), 51. First published, in French, in *Nouvelle Revue Française*, 19 (1 December 1922), pp. 751–56; it was solicited for *Vanity Fair* by the magazine's young managing editor, Edmund Wilson (see Wilson, *Letters on Literature and Politics 1912–1972*, ed. Elena Wilson [New York: Farrar, Straus and Giroux, 1977], p. 103).

SANDRA M. GILBERT ON
ELIOT'S MOURNING OF A FRIEND

That *The Waste Land* is not only elegiac in manner but more strictly in *mode* has already been argued by quite a few critics, including James Miller, Gregory Jay, and myself. In 1977, for instance, Miller offered a particularly interesting analysis of the efforts at elegiac resolution embodied in "What the Thunder Said," while in 1983 Jay noted that the "corpus of the elegy lies buried in *The Waste Land.*" Jay's reading was primarily Bloomian, with hardly any reference to the work's biographical context, but Miller's discussion, evolving out of his brilliant and still underappreciated *T. S. Eliot's Personal Waste Land*, drew on John Peter's 1952 hypothesis that the poem's central but repressed theme is its author's grief for a beloved male friend whom we now know to have been the young French medical student Jean Verdenal, killed in action at Gallipoli on May 2, 1915. [26] And by now, too, most Eliot scholars would concede that the death of Verdenal inspired in the writer of *The Waste Land* a personal and poetic crisis. Understanding the young Frenchman to have been "(so far as I could find out) ... mixed with the mud of Gallipoli," the poet himself plunged into the muck of a "rats' alley" where "the dead men lost their bones," and a waste land at whose center his dead friend is buried.[27]

Read as a dirge for Verdenal, therefore, *The Waste Land* becomes a kind of fragmented pastoral (or, more accurately, antipastoral) elegy, a work that both continues and, in response to severe personal *and* cultural shock, disrupts the tradition of a man mourning for a man that extends from Moschus [Greek pastoral poet, c. 150 B.C.] and Bion [the subject of a dirge believed to have been written by Moschus] to [Walt] Whitman and is also radically mutilated in Owen's "Strange Meeting" [an elegy a soldier writes for the man he killed, whom he meets in death with a tenderness he did not know when his enemy was alive]. Indeed, read in this way, Eliot's *Waste Land* may be considered a figure for No Man's Land itself, a ravaged terrain littered with the shards of the English elegy. Here, haunted not so much by the ghost as by the literal body of a dead comrade ("Those are pearls that were his eyes") whose *blutbruderschaft* had in a sense guaranteed his own identity, Eliot/Tiresias becomes himself an impassioned witness to the woes of a world shattered by (and for) the war's shattered armies of the night.

At the same time, because he is a mourner driven by precisely the need for consolation that impels the speakers of traditional elegies like those whose lineaments his poem explodes, the

Waste Land speaker deploys (albeit with considerable savagery) many conventional features of the pastoral elegy: the ironic discrepancy between nature's endurance as manifested in the returning spring and his own sense of mortal loss ("April is the cruelest month"); a consciousness that he speaks for, even while he is somehow set apart from, a community of mourners ("crowds of people walking round in a ring"); a feeling that the world which has survived his friend is itself debilitated by loss ("I had not thought death had undone so many"); a vision of the dead man journeying deeper into death ("He passed the stages of his age and youth / Entering the whirlpool"); a warning that such a fate is universal ("Consider Phlebas, who was once handsome and tall as you"); and an effort to confound death either by imagining resurrection ("a damp gust / Bringing rain") or by redefining the terror of mortality ("Shantih Shantih Shantih").[28]

But because Eliot has lost his friend to an unprecedentedly calamitous war and finds himself in a postwar deathscape where, as Freud put it, the "all-embracing patrimony [of Western culture is] disintegrated," he has only fragments of the pastoral elegy to shore against his ruin. Thus the muses, nymphs, envoys of nature, and spectral visitors who appear in most elegies to guide the sufferer toward consolation are here even more deformed than the dead double Owen encounters in the dull tunnel of *his* elegy. *Lycidas*'s "sisters of the sacred well" and *Adonais*'s (or *In Memoriam*'s) Urania become the parodic Madame Sosostris, the sinister Belladonna, and the vulgar Lil; Milton's and Shelley's nymphs (and *In Memoriam*'s radiant bride) metamorphose into the nymphs who have "now departed" with or without "the loitering heirs of city directors," into the bored typist, into the betrayed Thames daughters, and perhaps most horrifyingly, into the intransigently common "Mrs. Porter and her daughter," antiheroines of a bawdy ballad sung by Australian troops at Gallipoli, where Verdenal died; Whitman's bird victoriously singing "death's outlet song" becomes not just the hallucinatory "water-dripping" hermit thrush but also the raped nightingale who only says "jug jug" to "dirty ears"; and Whitman's comforting "Dark mother always gliding near with soft feet" dissolves into a disembodied "Murmur of maternal lamentation" or a ghastly woman, clearly figuring death, who draws "her long black hair out tight."

(...)

But if *The Waste Land* responds to the trauma of the war by fragmenting the pastoral elegy, it also retains within the text significant traces of what we might consider the deadly shell that shocked its author. Although the poem is usually seen as marked by the war in only the general way in which most postwar art was affected by a pervasive cultural disillusionment, Eliot's ostensibly "impersonal" document is specifically imprinted with wistful memories of Verdenal, with haunting references to Gallipoli, and with horrified allusions to the details of the battlefield, whose most gruesome particularities had been widely reported by the time the author began to write his poem. To be sure, as is the case with any great work, the imagery of *The Waste Land* is overdetermined, but even just a quick look at the text yields striking specifics.

Verdenal: it was the "cruel month" of April in which the poet's friendship with this *simpatico* young Frenchman, a lover of Wagner and Laforgue, seems to have truly flowered, as is evident from a letter of Eliot's to a cousin, from Verdenal's letters to Eliot, and from Eliot's single published reference to his Paris *ami*, apart from the dedications of early volumes. In a jubilant letter of 26 April 1911, Eliot wrote that "Paris has burst out ... into full spring: and it is such a revelation that I feel that I ought to make it known," adding that "M. Verdenal was in the garden and ... I threw a lump of sugar at him." [30]

On April 22, 1912, a year later, Verdenal wrote Eliot in Cambridge to tell him that "Vous me fûtes particulierement évoqué par le contact de ce paysage senti ensemble": that Eliot was particularly evoked for him by the verdant landscape that they had admired, appreciated, *felt* together ("*senti ensemble*"). And in a previous letter, he quoted a passage from Gide's *Paludes* (1895) filled with yearning to return to "that place I know, where in darkened ... water, the *leaves* of bygone years are still steeping and softening—the leaves of *adorable springtimes*" (*L* 32; emphasis mine).

Finally, decades later, in April 1934, Eliot wrote in *The Criterion*, in a rare personal moment, about his own poignant memory of "a sentimental sunset [and] a friend coming across the Luxembourg gardens in the late afternoon, waving a branch of lilac, a friend who was later (so far as I could find out) to be mixed with the mud of Gallipoli." [31]

(...)

And it was on this historically resonant yet ultimately "savage" and "desolate" peninsula, this "arid rocky" finger of Europe reaching toward Asia, that Verdenal was cited for his heroism on April 30, 1915, when "scarcely recovered from pleurisy [he] did not hesitate to spend much of the night in the water up to his waist helping to evacuate the wounded by sea" (*TS* 21). And it was in this liminal place between land and sea, rock and shadow, that the young French doctor was killed in action, again tending the wounded, two days later.

Details of his death, and of the battlefield on which he died, may have at first been difficult to obtain, but as Eliot admitted in his comment in the *Criterion*, the poet sought to find out as much as he could. Much of what he understood to have happened was surely gleaned from information that gradually emerged about combat conditions. He would surely have read Masefield's book—a narrative by a literary colleague, after all— and he would have learned from other accounts, too. Learned, for instance, that on the Gallipoli peninsula the "labyrinths of trenches" had sardonic names like "Dublin Castle, Half Moon Street" or (I would add) "rats' alley" (*FT* 193). That the Anzacs sang bawdily about Mrs. Porter and her daughter. That the dead men lost their bones because they so often went unburied. That queer sardonic rats were everywhere. That the jolly old rain gave no relief. And later, long after the war, that on the Gallipoli peninsula and elsewhere the (re)"Burial of the Dead," those never properly buried and those only (as it were) temporarily buried, became a significant issue, with, as Jay Winter reminds us, in the early 'twenties hundreds of thousands of dead soldiers being *dug up* (like the corpse in *The Waste Land*) and posthumously "demobbed"—that is, sent home for reburial (*SM* 22–30).

Notes

26. In what has since become a classic of literary censorship, the poet's solicitors had Peter's original essay suppressed, but Peter's argument is still much the most incisive statement of what might be considered the text's covert "plot," for whether or not one would choose to claim that the speaker of *The Waste Land* had "fallen completely," even "irretrievably," in love, it is clear that *an* "object of his love was a young man." See John Peter, "A New Interpretation of the *Waste Land*," in *Essays in Criticism*, 2 (1952), 242–66; also James Miller, *T. S. Eliot's Personal Waste Land: Exorcism of the Demons* (University Park, Pa., 1977), hereafter cited in text as *TS*; and also Gregory Jay, *T. S. Eliot and the Poetics of Literary History* (Baton Rouge, La., 1983), pp. 156–62. My own earlier discussion of *The Waste Land* as fragmented elegy appears in *Sexchanges*, pp. 310–14.

27. Eliot's comment about Verdenal was made in a review of Henri Massis, *Evocations*, that appeared in the *Criterion*, April 1934; the poet remembered "a friend coming across the Luxembourg Gardens in the late afternoon, waving a branch of lilac, a friend who was later (so far as I could find out) to be mixed with the mud of Gallipoli"; for further commentary see Miller, *Eliot's Personal Waste Land*, p, 19 and *passim*. For other analyses of the relationship see George Watson, "Quest for a Frenchman," *The Sewanee Review*, 84 (1976), 465–75, and John T. Mayer, *T. S. Eliot's Silent Voices* (New York, 1989), pp. 199–202. Without entering into details about what some commentators have scathingly called "the homosexual interpretation of *The Waste Land*," I must confess that I myself have long thought the argument about Verdenal's significance to Eliot is incontrovertible. It was to "Jean Verdenal/1889–1915," after all (as Miller and others have reminded us), that the 1917 *Prufrock and Other Observations*, the 1920 *Ara Vos Prec*, and the 1925 *Poems: 1909–1925* were dedicated, with the addition in 1925 of the identifying tag *mort aux Dardanelles* and the telling epigraph from Canto 21 of *The Purgatorio* that declares "Now you are able to comprehend the quantity of love that warms me toward you, / When I forget our emptiness / Treating shades as if they were solid." And it seems almost certain that it was of Verdenal as well as of his own unhappy marriage that Eliot was thinking when he so famously remarked that his ostensibly impersonal cultural document was really only the product of "a personal ... grouse against life."

28. A number of the points I make here and in the next few paragraphs are drawn from *Sexchanges* .

30. T. S. Eliot, *The Letters of T. S. Eliot, Volume 1 1898–1922*, ed. Valerie Eliot (New York, 1988), p. 18; hereafter cited in text as *L*.

31. See n. 27 above.

MICHAEL LEVENSON ON ELIOT'S VIEWS OF POSTWAR LONDON

When Eliot settled in London, he moved steadily into an infatuation with his new home. "I like London better than before"—"I like London very well"—"I have been to a cubist tea"—"I want to live in London"—"I love to be in London" (*LOTSE*, 55, 57, 77, 107, 122). Still, within the chanting, crooning enthusiasm, he remained acutely conscious of the strains on a foreigner. It's no surprise that his affection for the city grew in proportion to the successful spinning of a social web. He repeatedly counts the number of friends in those early months; he needs those friends because, as he later put it, "getting recognized in English letters is like breaking open a safe—for an American" (*LOTSE*, 392).

By 1919 Eliot can boast that he has "more *influence* on English letters than any other American has ever had, unless it be Henry James. I know a great many people, but there are many more who would like to know me ..." The possibility of returning to the United States lingers: Charles W. Eliot, the ex-President of Harvard, asks how his kinsman "can forego the privilege of living in the genuine American atmosphere—a bright atmosphere of freedom and hope" (*LOTSE*, 323). But whatever the attractions of freedom, London has the allure of power: "if one is to do anything in literature this is the best place to be," and this because "London imposes her acceptance of a man's work on all the English speaking world and ... accepts no other standard than her own" (*LOTSE*, 107, 102). On this point Eliot is clear, convinced, and self-delighted: London is the imperial capital of culture, and to break open its safe is to uncover riches that can be redeemed in any literary market.

The "safe" is, of course, a resonant figure of speech for a young banker, resonant but not surprising, because we certainly misread both Eliot's modernity and his urbanity if we ignore his role as a practitioner of economics, working amid various subtle currencies.[3] What appears in one guise as the question of war reparations, shows itself in another as a problem in the economies of literary reputation. From the start of his London life he understands and accepts the material conditions of success, the economy of reputation. It is essential, he concludes, that a writer "should establish solid connections with at least one important paper" (*LOTSE*, 358)—and there follows the coldly unsentimental insight:

There are only two ways in which a writer can become important—to write a great deal, and have his writings appear everywhere, or to write very little ... I write very little, and I should not become more powerful by increasing my output. My reputation in London is built upon one small volume of verse, and is kept up by printing two or three more poems in a year. The only thing that matters is that these should be perfect in their kind, so that each should be an event. (*LOTSE*, 358)

This is a canny exercise in what might fairly be called cynical literary reason.[4] It suggests that Eliot's banker's understanding of writing markets led him to administer his reputation carefully within a robustly modernized urban culture.[5] He will write that he is intent to keep his book of criticism short: "I want it small," he writes, "in order to make it a single distinct blow" (*LOTSE*, 355). In choosing to follow the little way, the terse way, Eliot acknowledges the power of cultural mystery, of the reticent perfectionist, who locks the safe he has broken open, and who, to change figures, creates hunger by feeding the public so sparingly. At the same time he opens a connection between the conditions of reputation and the forms of literary experiment practiced in those early London years. The suppression of a narrative continuity that was still flickering in "Prufrock" and "Portrait of a Lady," the burnishing of smaller fragments, the violent shift in attention between verse paragraphs, the movement to the greater difficulty of the quatrain poems, "Gerontion," and climactically *The Waste*

Land—all this occurs within the complex cultural universe that Eliot seeks to command through the economic resources of the "single distinct blow," whether it take the form of a short critical book or a self-standing poetic conceit: "A woman drew her long black hair out tight." [6]

Through the grimness of the war years, Eliot sought and quickly felt the mastery of the imperial literary summit. In the spring of 1919 he writes, "I am getting to know and be known by all the intelligent or important people in letters" (*LOTSE*, 285). And yet through the course of that year Eliot felt a sudden dissolution of the carefully prepared edifice of mastery. The wartime metropolis had been a depleted city, where literary activity had been reduced to a low simmer. Even as some modernists fought and died—T. E. Hulme and Gaudier-Brzeska among them—those who stayed home in London had found an urban culture small and pliable enough to yield to literary activism. Surely it's telling that the great moment of crisis in Eliot's work coincides with the recovery of peace. The postwar metropolis became the saturated city again, but for Eliot the vigorous city was a new difficulty. "London has never been so full," writes Vivien Eliot, "the crowds are so enormous, everywhere, in the streets and public places, theatres restaurants ... one sees Americans at every turn" (*LOTSE*, 265).

Written so soon after the carnage of the war, the poem has naturally been understood as an engagement with the civilization of violence. But a burden of this argument is that *The Waste Land* needs to be located within the immediate surround of the postwar city, the city cursed not by military violence, but by hectic peace. It's the city of the dead, as we have always known, but these are peculiar corpses: they twitch so spasmodically. Eliot's London letters for *The Dial* and his private correspondence describe "the putrescence of English literature" (*LOTSE*, 431), but the accumulating picture is one of a seething putrescence, a frantic routine. The drafts of "The Fire Sermon" are searing.

London, the swarming life you kill and breed,
Huddled between the concrete and the sky;

London, your people is bound upon the wheel!
Phantasmal gnomes, burrowing in brick and stone and steel!
(*TWL*, 31, 106–7, 112–13).

It's the roiling capital of peace that consumes Eliot, the boom town that haunts him as the war never did: the noisy, swarming town, not conscious enough to know that it's dead. The urban destruction in *The Waste Land*—London Bridge falling down, the collapsing towers of the European capitals—takes on a peculiar valence: a tone of perceptible relief that lives within the catastrophe.[7] What the poem both dreads and desires is the annihilation of the city as apparatus, what Eliot calls "the postwar machinery of life" with its "horrible waste," the city as the relentless wheel (*LOTSE*, 410).

2.

John Maynard Keynes published *The Economic Consequences of the Peace* in 1919 as a bitter polemic against the Peace Treaty agreed at the Paris conference. Having attended the conference as an official of the British Treasury, Keynes was witness to the working of power at its most lofty summit. What he saw was the fatal emptiness of the grand Parisian bargain. Gazing at the faces of the world's great leaders, of Wilson and Clemenceau, he came to doubt whether they "were really faces at all and not the tragi-comic masks of some strange drama or puppet-show."[8] "The nerve center of the European system" was haunted by "dreadful specters."

"Paris was a nightmare and everyone there was morbid. A sense of impending catastrophe overhung the frivolous scene; the futility and smallness of man before the great events confronting him; the mingled significance and unreality of the decisions; levity, blindness, insolence, confused cries from without ... " (*ECP*, 5)

More than Jessie Weston, more than *The Golden Bough*, *The Economic Consequences of the Peace* anticipates the ghostly modality of *The Waste Land*, the spectral insight into the fictions of modernity. Keynes's Paris is the unreal city of peace:

there are no living people there, only the heavy masks of insubstantial men, flapping the artificial wings of leadership. Since the work of Eleanor Cook we've had reason to ponder the connection between Eliot and Keynes, and reason to connect Keynes' book to Eliot's labor at Lloyds Bank, where he described himself as "dealing alone with all the debts and claims of the bank under the various Peace Treaties" (*LOTSE*, 451).[9] But *The Economic Consequences of the Peace* must be read as more than a textual impetus to the writing of *The Waste Land*; it must be seen as a canny instrument for stitching the relations of politics, economics and poetry at an uncanny juncture.

Power absconditus—that is the savage Keynesian insight: those who have been entrusted with the world's fate have withdrawn into the fantasy of an untenable peace. It is all like Tolstoy, shrieks Keynes, it's like Hardy's *The Dynasts*, this spectacle of "events marching on to their fated conclusion uninfluenced and unaffected by the cerebrations of Statesmen in Council" (*ECP*, 6).

Here is the first cold perception that we need to bring to the politics of *The Waste Land*, exactly the perception of *power absconditus*. There was an Archduke who once took Marie out on a sled. There was a Coriolanus, now broken. There were loitering heirs of city directors, now departed, having left no addresses. There was a Fisher King. All these powers have receded, creating a landscape in which fearful selves are left to wander, at the mercy of forces no longer governed by once formidable authorities, Kings and Generals, Directors and Dukes.

And yet when big power absconds, it leaves little power behind. Such is its genius.[10] The epigraph from *Heart of Darkness*, discarded in the late stages of revision, belongs to this pattern of abandonment. Kurtz is yet another recent leader whose recession will abandon events to their own blind course. And yet we know that the agony of Kurtz's retrospection—his horror, his horror—is both a crisis in social power and a crisis of subjectivity. No doubt the allure of Conrad's Kurtz for Eliot, as an exemplary, epigraphic figure, depended on the productive confusion of realms: personal agony indistinguishable from political catastrophe.

The Waste Land, with all its toppled towers of authority, displays power persisting. It persists in the opportunities within the zone of personal intimacy, in the micro-power of intersubjectivity. The barbarous king who rudely forced Philomela is the terrible figure for the politics of intimacy, power between bodies, whose effects are written throughout the poem. Eliot envisions the local dyad, two flailing, flirting subjects, as a little system of submission and hierarchy, obedience and control. As the glimpsed idyll in the poem's final movements puts it, "your heart would have responded/ Gaily, when invited, beating obedient/ To controlling hands" (*TWL*, 146, 420–22). Give, sympathize, and control—these are the overcharged imperatives of regulated subjectivity.

"It is terrible to be alone with another person,"—so Eliot had written (in "The Death of the Duchess," *TWL*, 105, 25), and the ferocity of this insight is everywhere abrasive in *The Waste Land*. Two people make their own politics. Whether they give or control, either in silence or in howling eroticism, the mere human pair are already expert in the administration of power. "What is to be done?" demanded Lenin. In the drawing-room politics of *The Waste Land* this becomes, "What shall we do to-morrow? What shall we ever do?" (*TWL*, 138, 133–34) All through the poem runs the appalling compound of bottomless demand ("Stay with me," "Speak to me," 138, 111–12) and endless refusal ("I can't bear to look at you," 146). This is what Beckett will exploit and exhaust: this scene of two creatures alone, begging, clutching, biting, tickling, loving, loathing, without even the solace of a frame around the misery.

What the micro-politics of intimacy lacks is a world to inhabit, a society stretching out around the desperate dyad, a political context within which helpless subjectivity might orient itself. In a universe where "each man fixed his eyes before his feet" (*TWL*, 136, 65), even the intelligibility of space disappears. You trace the steps of the one in front of you, or you find yourself in a closed car; you follow the current of the city streets, or you drift with the river; but you never assemble a coherent or stable milieu that might be called an "outer world." These grammatical subjects can finally do little more than testify to their victimage: "I read much of the night" (*TWL*, 135, 18); "After the event/ He wept" (143, 297–98); "I can connect/ Nothing with nothing" (143, 301–2).

And how could she? How could she connect her suffering to the political incoherence of *The Waste Land* moment—of 1921, that year of "incessant strain and stress", a year of starvation in Russia, of Irish militancy, of unprecedented unemployment, of a coal strike in Britain from April to June described as "the greatest dispute and cessation of work ever recorded in any country."[11] For figures in *The Waste Land* the legitimacy of government is only a memory, not a frame or a background or a confirming world picture.[12]

3.

The disappearance of the background of conviction, the dissolution of a world-picture—Keynes is at his most searching when he describes their loss. We never noticed, he writes, that what we took as natural and permanent, namely, the political life of the West in the fifty years before the war, was in fact "intensely unusual, unstable, complicated, unreliable, [and] temporary." The end of the war has exposed the truth: that what Europe understood as the order of things was a recent contrivance whose collapse leaves us on a "sandy and false foundation" (*ECP*, 3). The great rise of European capital depended on *naturalizing* an artifice as something "normal, certain, and permanent" (*ECP*, 12). But now Europe must live with the dissolution of the norm, the decay of the natural.

What happens then to politics when its "nature" can no longer mystify, when the great statesmen stand revealed as puppets, when potent events overwhelm paltry agents, and when paltry agents are left to exercise power on their own? The answer for Keynes, and no less for Eliot, is that politics devolves into an economics, where economics is the name for the play of interests and desires when they are no longer veiled (or constrained) by the theatrics of political deception. The system of Europe had depended on the "double bluff," by which the great capitalists agreed to invest, not to consume, and workers were persuaded that they somehow had a stake in the wealth of others. After the war the bluff has been exposed; politics descends into the unsentimental truths of economics, the truth of the power in material interests.

In its crowds on the bridge, in its hooded hordes, *The Waste Land* tersely acknowledges the class basis of the disenchanted postwar world, but just as the London crowd resolves into Stetson, so the poem makes its sharp turn toward individuals, and public concerns gather around personal pronouns: my ruins, my lands. But in this Waste Land to remain alone is exactly not to escape the politico/economic crisis of those first postwar years, the crisis Keynes identified with the insight of Lenin, who thought that "the best way to destroy the Capitalist system was to debauch [its] currency." A "debauch" is just what the *Times* called it, this period of startling inflation built on the quicksand of rising prices. The cost of living rose month by month, climbing to a peak at the end of 1920, and the difficulty wasn't scarcity of goods: the problem was "scandalous profiteering," middlemen with ample supplies unwilling to bring prices down, intent to enjoy, for as long as they could, the artificial boom.[13] The government was seen as helpless—bands of shoppers, hoodless hordes, took matters into their own hands, organizing boycotts against the profiteers. When the Eliots looked for a new flat in 1920, they found that the "fantastic" rents were running "from two to four times what we pay now" (*LOTSE*, 406, 390). The sagging poet complained to his mother that though his salary had risen to 500 pounds, "which would have seemed a fortune ... four years ago" (*LOTSE*, 353), now it is worth scarcely more than 250 pounds.

The notorious young man carbuncular in *The Waste Land* is, notably, a small house agent's clerk, who (the drafts explain) "flits" from "flat to flat" with clients like the Eliots (*TWL*, 45, 157–58). He is a case worker in the inflationary epidemic—a middleman within the system of profiteering. If he has a bold stare like a Bradford millionaire, that is because in the city of flowing money, numbers now change their meaning. As Keynes caustically put it, "Where we spent millions before the war, we have now learnt that we can spend hundreds of millions and apparently not suffer for it" (*ECP*, 4).

As for the clerk's metropolitan bride, the typist home at teatime, she has already led a semi-lustrous life in Eliot's correspondence, where in describing the world of Lloyds Bank, he had written, "I have half of a room, two girls, and half of a typist" (*LOTSE*, 232), and then goes on to explain the problem with typists. The trouble is that some of them "don't have to work:" they just "want something to do" (*LOTSE*, 204). In *The Waste Land*, of course, this turns into the something-to-do of sexuality. The end of the war brought the arrival of single women in public places, on the bus and in the squares. Peter Walsh in *Mrs. Dalloway* returns to London from India and swoons before the women on the street: "even the poorest dressed better than five years ago surely; and to his eye the fashions had never been so becoming; the long black cloaks; the slimness, the elegance, and then the delicious and apparently universal habit of paint ... this taking out a stick of rouge or a powder-puff, and making up in public."[14] Eliot himself has known the subterranean tie between London and libido. Several years earlier he had described "one of those nervous sexual attacks which I suffer from when alone in a city ... One walks about the street with one's desires, and one's refinement rises up like a wall whenever opportunity approaches" (*LOTSE*, 75). But it's in the period of the twenties that the sexual heightening becomes conspicuous and inescapable; it appears as its own form of inflation, product of and counterpart to the inflation in prices, incomes and rents; and it appears up and down the social ladder.

> He's been in the army four years, he wants a good time,
> And if you don't give it him, there's others will, I said.
> Oh is there, she said. (*TWL*, 138–39, 148–50)

And, there is. That is the economic insight, the insight into a fevered economy, a sexual economy where there is more money chasing more bodies; in an apt Keynesian aphorism: "the war has disclosed the possibility of consumption to all and the vanity of abstinence to many" (*ECP*, 22). Or: "Others can pick and choose if you can't" (*TWL*, 139, 154).

Costing more and offering less, sex and commerce entwine in the city of raging peace. When the clerk and the typist clutch, fidget, and discharge, they perform their desires at the intersection point of this double coercion: money and libido. Mr. Eugenides may be unshaven but his traffic in currants yields enough cash for a lurid weekend. Those heirs to banking directorships may not yet have come into their plush offices on Threadneedle Street, but their silk handkerchiefs and cigarettes can still beguile the nymphs on the upper Thames. Such figures are the postwar successors to Fisher Kings and Archdukes, dispersed modern powers who can ride the crest of easy money. When "Death by Water" records the forgetting of the "profit and loss," it not only suggests a transfiguring death, it enacts the poem's own disengagement with bad currencies.

Notes

3. Lawrence Rainey has given the decisive account of the economic life of early modernism. See his richly detailed narrative of the negotiations leading to the publication of *The Waste Land*. "The Price of Modernism: Publishing *The Waste Land*," in *T. S. Eliot: The Modernist in History*, ed. Ronald Bush (Cambridge: Cambridge University Press, 1991), 91–133.

4. See Peter Sloterdijk, *Critique of Cynical Reason*, trans. Michael Eldred (Minneapolis: University of Minnesota Press, 1987).

5. Leonard Diepeveen discusses Eliot's management of his reputation through the active construction of an audience responsive to his forms of difficulty. Diepeveen reconstructs Eliot's tactic of creating "a small, qualified audience of good readers for modern writing. They form part of a small group who are willing to undergo the hard work and training required for reading modern writing, which is difficult, but necessarily so. The purpose of this narrowing down is not first of all to exclude readers (although it certainly does do that), for the maligned audience is not present. Rather, it is to encourage a small group of readers in a tendency that was encouraged by the sorts of magazines they read: to imagine themselves as part of a professional elite, as included in the appreciators of good writing, writing that looks remarkably like *The Waste Land*." "'I Can Have More Than Enough Power to Satisfy Me:' T. S. Eliot's Construction of His Audience," *Marketing Modernisms: Self-Promotion, Canonization,*

Rereading, ed. Kevin J. H. Dettmar and Stephen Watt (Ann Arbor: University of Michigan Press, 1996), 52.

6. T. S. Eliot, *The Waste Land: A Facsimile and Transcript of the Original Drafts*, ed. Valerie Eliot (New York: Harcourt Brace Jovanovich, 1971), 145, ln 377. Hereafter the work is abbreviated in the text as *TWL* followed by page and line number.

7. In Kenner's well-known argument, the evolution of the poem runs from the city of Dryden in the early drafts to the catastrophic anti-metropolitan tableau of "What the Thunder Said." The "center had become the urban apocalypse, the great City dissolved into a desert where voices sang from exhausted wells ..." Hugh Kenner, "The Urban Apocalypse," *Eliot in His Time*, ed. A. Walton Litz (Princeton: Princeton University Press, 1973), 46.

8. John Maynard Keynes, *The Economic Consequences of the Peace* (New York: Harcourt, Brace & Howe, 1920); hereafter abbreviated in the text as *ECP*.

9. Eleanor Cook notes of Keynes's book that it is "contemporary with the poem; its sheds light on some of the allusions in *The Waste Land*, ties the poem to post-World-War-I history, and incidentally relates Eliot's work at Lloyds Bank to his poetry." She further observes that "the phrasing in *The Economic Consequences of the Peace* evokes an apocalyptic foreboding, and sense of nightmare very like that in *The Waste Land*." "T. S. Eliot and the Carthaginian Peace," *ELH* 46 (1979): 347–48.

10. Here, of course, see Foucault on the filiations and imbrications of Power. Michel Foucault, *Discipline and Punish: The Birth of the Prison*, trans. Alan Sheridan (New York: Random House, 1979).

11. *Times*, 31 December 1921, 6.

12. The disorienting political geography of Eliot's postwar world is captured well by Cook, who unfolds the suggestions within the analogy between London after World War I and Rome after the Punic Wars. She invokes Augustine's gloomy account of Roman decadence: "after the destruction of Carthage there came the highest pitch of discord, greed, ambition, and all the evils which generally spring up in times of prosperity" ("T. S. Eliot and the Carthaginian Peace," 350). David Roessel locates Mr. Eugenides within the context of the postwar struggle between Turkey and Greece over the national identity of Smyrna, noting that "Trade with Smyrna played an important role in discussions over the city in the English newspapers ..." See "'Mr. Eugenides, The Smyrna Merchant,' and Post-War Politics in *The Waste Land*," *Journal Of Modern Literature* 50.1 (Summer 1989): 173.

13. *Times*, 7 September 1921, 7.

14. Virginia Woolf, *Mrs. Dalloway* (Harmondsworth: Penguin, 1964), 79–80.

Juan A. Suárez on the Meaning of the Gramophone

The gramophone is heard in a prominent, if squalid, segment of *The Waste Land*. It appears in part three ("The Fire Sermon"), in one of the emblematic moments of modern degradation which the poem seeks at once to portray and to overcome. This is the sexual encounter between a jaded typist and a "young man carbuncular"—"A small house agent's clerk ... on whom assurance sits / As a silk hat on a Bradford millionaire."[5] Their tryst is prefaced by elliptical views of the city (the polluted Thames and its banks; the bustle of traffic); invocations of death and decay; and by a brief passage, "under the brown fog of a winter noon," in which the ever-mutating first-person narrator receives an ambiguous invitation from a Mr. Eugenides, "the Smyrna merchant": "Asked me in demotic French / To luncheon at the Cannon Street Hotel" (*WL* 208, 209, 212–13).[6] These contemporary scenes are haunted by gadgets, mass-produced objects, and industrial landscapes which render the present mechanical, jarring, lifeless, and disenchanted. Take, for example, "the sound of horns and motors" (*WL* 197) in city streets; the "empty bottles, sandwich papers, / Silk handkerchiefs, cardboard boxes, cigarette ends / Or other testimony of summer nights" (*WL* 177–79) on the river banks; the "gashouse" by "the dull canal," where the rats scurry over moldy bones (*WL* 189–90); or the customs forms which fill Mr. Eugenides's pockets (*WL* 211).

As one more vignette of present-day decadence, the exhausted rendezvous between the typist and her suitor also unfolds under emblems of industrial modernity. It takes place in the early evening, after work, when "the human engine waits / Like a taxi throbbing, waiting" (*WL* 216–17). Home from the office, the typist lights up her stove, tidies up, and "lays out food in tins" (*WL* 223). Presently, her guest arrives "with one bold stare" (*WL* 232). Once dinner is over, he makes his advance, which meets with neither resistance nor encouragement. The encounter is unspirited; the insistently mechanical rhythm of the lines underlines its somnambulistic quality. After he leaves, she remains prey to automatism and machine conditioning:

> She turns and looks a moment in the glass,
> Hardly aware of her departed lover;
> Her brain allows one half-formed thought to pass....
> Paces about her room again, alone,
> She smoothes her hair with automatic hand,
> And puts a record on the gramophone.
> (*WL* 249–51, 254–56)

The canned music of the gramophone clinches the mechanical squalor of the entire scene and comes to stand for the vulgarity and disenchantment of contemporary existence.

(...)

[In] *The Waste Land*, the gramophone's sound closes the poem's bleak, necromantic first half. Shortly afterward begin the intimations of rebirth and redemption. Already the following stanza evokes "the pleasant whining of a mandoline," heard in a pub on Lower Thames Street and the neo-classical splendor of the church of Magnus Martyr, by Christopher Wren (*WL* 261, 264). The folk performance and the "Ionian white and gold" of the monument offset debased modern existence and its accoutrements. The following section, "Death by Water," contains a poignant *memento mori*; and in the closing fragment, "What the Thunder Said," the scorched, rocky earth breaks into new life. The oppressive present is obscurely redeemed then. Modern city scenes are replaced by timeless landscapes, while the shrill sounds of contemporary life are displaced by the rumble of thunder; by mythic invocations drawn from the *Upanishads*; and by literary allusions ranging from antiquity to the Renaissance. In the end, the choral voice of tradition drowns the artificial sounds of modernity—among them, the mechanical grinding of the gramophone—and restores to life a hard-won, new organicity. And yet I will try to show that, if one listens closely, it becomes apparent that the sounds of tradition are played back by a gramophone. The organic, mystic unity with which, it is generally agreed, the poem ends, is entirely dependent on it. The gramophone's prerecorded sound is the condition of possibility for the entire work. In his attempt to modernize the idiom of modern poetry, Eliot was shaping an old medium in the image of a new one.[10]

(...)

Although jazz (like ragtime, its predecessor) was primarily a live musical form, its boom coincided with that of the gramophone. It was dependent on it for its diffusion and full impact. Jazzing and ragging, like all parody, depend for their effect on knowledge of the original being transformed. They presupposed a stock of musical references shared by listener and performer, just like Eliot's poem presupposed the accessibility of the literary archive—played back as a mélange of broken sound bites. In addition, jazz's strategies of defamiliarization and parody were favored by the distance that recordings created between the music itself, performers, and audiences. As music streams from metal tubes, horns, and pulsating membranes, it loses its aura—its uniqueness and unrepeatability—and loosens its ties to the personality, the genius, the body and the nerves of the performer or composer. It becomes more controllable by the listener than live music could ever be. Moreover, canned music is forced to commingle, indeed to compete, with the din of street life—"the sound of horns and motors." The performance is no longer bracketed off from daily routine; it may now happen any time—as when the typist in *The Waste Land* freshens up after "stooping to folly." Once all types of music are intimately woven with the ordinary, they appear ripe for parody and appropriation.

Like music, literature in the electronic age is subjected to a similar fall into the ordinary. And this not only because, at least since romanticism, literary mimesis has been making the quotidian its main focus of interest. Literature loses some of its sacredness and solemnity when writing notes down the automatic speech of the world and thus imitates electronic receivers and transmitters. According to McLuhan, the electronic media have a leveling effect (*UM* 247). Once the channels are open, they carry any and all sounds, those of time-tested tradition as well as—mixed in with—the most ephemeral and mundane. A reporter present at the first demonstrations of Edison's phonograph at the offices of *Scientific American* put it as follows: "With charming impartiality it [the phonograph] will express itself in the divine strains of a lyric goddess, or use the startling vernacular of a street Arab."[34] The gramophone's nondiscriminating ear then explodes the queen's English and places it in open competition with all other dialects and inflections, and with sheer noise (*DN* 233). Hence in *The Waste Land* gramophonics blows up stylistic uniformity, and with it, extant cultural hierarchies. That is why Shakespeare and pub talk share the same frequencies; or why the *Upanishads*, Pope, and Dante blend in with jazz rhythms or the drone of city crowds; or why Ophelia and Lil, the cockney working-class woman, touch hands.

As do Eliot and the typist. She is, after all, the poem's originator; the one who gives Eliot his gramophone—electronic memory, language transmitter, verse generator—and his desire. She is ultimately the stand-in for authorship in the machine age—she, the medium who takes dictation; the conduit of voices, discourses, and noise which travel through her as through information channels; the one in whom language is detached from "the spirit" and its acrobatics and entangled in technological networks. One could say that in his attempt to modernize the idiom of modern poetry, Eliot grafted onto an old medium the "minor," marginal vernaculars of modernity: the language of women, of machines, of popular culture. The language of those with no *proper* language.

Notes

5. T. S. Eliot, *The Waste Land*, lines 231–34; hereafter cited in text as *WL* by line number, in *The Complete Poems and Plays, 1909–1950* (New York, 1971), pp. 37–55; hereafter cited in text as *CPP.*

6. It seems to me the reader is invited to cringe at the invitation ("in demotic *French*"! no less), whose placement reveals that, for Eliot, this kind of homoerotic possibility sounds the depths of contemporary

decadence. For another example of Eliot's homophobic anxieties, see Peter Ackroyd, *T. S. Eliot: A Life* (London, 1984), pp. 309–10.

10. This inverts somewhat Marshall McLuhan's idea that the content of a new medium is always an older one: the content of radio is the written word; of cinema, the theater; of television, both the cinema and the radio, and so on. See his *Understanding Media: The Extensions of Man* (New York, 1964); hereafter cited in text as *UM*.

34. Anonymous, "Mr. Edison's New Wonder," *Harper's Weekly*, 30 March 1878, 31; cited in Martin W. Laforse and James A. Drake, *Popular Culture and American Life* (Chicago, 1981), p. 3.

SHAWN R. TUCKER ON ANXIETY IN *THE WASTE LAND*

Temporal markers in *The Waste Land* create the poem's sense of a permanent pending. The bartender's repeated warning, "Hurry up please it's time," and the hints of Marvel's "To His Coy Mistress" give a sense of urgency closer to the proddings of Dante's demons than any conventional temporal progression. This sense of anxious urgency is reiterated in lines like "And still she cried, and still the world pursues," and "Here one can neither stand nor lie nor sit" (102, 340). Anne Wright points out that even the confounded verb tenses and "the quasi-adjectival use of the present participle[,] with or without modal verbs, register anxiety over death and rebirth, stasis and change" (165). She adds that the preponderance and "triumph of the present participle as verb-form within the poem denies to it certain completion" (165). Wright notes that such participles dominate the opening lines; of the first seven lines, five end with a present participle set apart by a comma. April's cruel "breeding, mixing, and stirring" match Tiresias's "throbbing waiting," and St. Augustine and the Buddha's lamentation of the vast "Burning burning burning burning" (*The Waste Land* 217, 308). As "The Fire Sermon" ends, these four tolling present participles are followed by St. Augustine's prayer of thanksgiving and hope, "O Lord Thou pluckest me out." Yet this sentiment first seems to crack and deteriorate in the next line, "O Lord Thou pluckest," followed by the typographical emptiness, and then the final understated, tragic, and liminoid "burning" (309, 310, 311).

The Waste Land is also haunted by a phantasmagoria of liminoid figures. The caged Cumaean Sibyl, afflicted by both the prophetic vision of pain and the inability to die, hangs suspended in a terrible, liminoid u-topos. In a similar manner, Tiresias witnesses and vicariously suffers while he is "throbbing between two lives," including that of a male and a female, and that of one who dwells "among the lowest of the dead" in both London and ancient Thebes (218, 246). Also suspended in a terrible transition is Marie, who looks back to an idealized past, as she seeks to escape an unbearable present. Even the disillusionment of the "hyacinth girl" betrays a similar tension: "I was neither / Living nor dead, and I knew nothing, / Looking into the heart of light, the silence" (39–41). Reduced to silence, she hangs between life and death. The disjointed "conversation" among the upper-class couple in "A Game of Chess" climaxes with this frantic interrogative: "Are you alive, or not?" (127). The sense of being "neither living nor dead" is nowhere more evident than in the mass of faceless figures who "flow over London Bridge" (62). Eliot's allusion is not to the carefully arranged damned in Dante's *Inferno*, but to those in the vestibule of hell or limbo. Dante describes those figures as "wretches never born and never dead" who "circling and circling" seem to "scorn all pause" (43). Those in limbo cannot go to heaven, and hell "will not receive them since the wicked might feel some glory over them" (43). These lost souls are denied "even a name" (43). Like other figures in the poem, these flowing hordes, suspended between life and death, experience a liminoid existence.

Besides the permanent pending created by temporal markers, present participles, and liminoid figures, Eliot's work focusses on the unresolved middle of all of the poem's mythic patterns. In the Osiris myth, any final meaningful or redemptive telos seems highly doubtful at best. The speaker in the "Burial of the Dead" asks Stetson if the corpse "has begun to sprout" and "will it bloom this year," but a blurring of narrator, subject, and reader comes before a reply is made (72). Yet the vulgarized

Osiris, buried in an English garden, resembles the victim of a pulp-crime novel, not a regenerative life force. The focus on the still-unresolved middle of the myth characterizes the way the poem engages the journey to Emmaus as well. The fourth stanza of "What the Thunder Said" alludes to the trip taken by two disciples and the disguised and resurrected Jesus. The moment depicted is before Jesus's revelation to them, yet here one of the travellers wonders about the identity of an evasive if not illusory third person. This subject's very nature and gender are left ambiguous. In addition, Eliot's note about the passage superimposes on that subject an allusion to the hallucinations of Antarctic explorers, which attaches even more instability to the mythic journey toward revelation or redemption. As the travellers are left questioning the very existence of the third figure, any ultimate epiphany promised by the mythic journey is, in the poem, forever deferred.

The fragmentary elements of the Grail quest are presented out of their conventional order, and this not only destroys any sense of continuity, but, like the journey to Emmaus and the Osiris myth, it also perpetually defers resolution. The first allusion comes in the context of foul fete with Sweeney, Mrs. Porter, and her daughter by the Thames. Next to the bawdy song used to portray this trio, Eliot places the concluding line of Verlaine's rendition of the Parsifal story: "Et O ces voix d'enfants, chantant dans la coupole!" (202). This striking contrast vulgarizes the quest by association, yet it also points toward its possible resolution, however premature the celebration. In the poem's final section, at the end of the mythic journey, the knight finds a "decayed hole," "tumbled graves," and a chapel that is "only the wind's home" (386, 388, 389). The ambiguous resolution of that quest, like the other mythic journeys, leaves both knight and reader suspended in an indeterminate "no where."

The Waste Land, like Pound's "Kongo Roux," mocks any humanistic utopia or "new Athens" at the same time that the poem, like Picabia's "Monument to Latin Stupidity," subverts conceits of teleological progression. Eliot's work undermines utopianism and temporal, psychological, or mythic progression by dissolving historical locations and subjects into one vast liminoid experience. The last seventeen lines of "The Burial of the Dead" display an "Unreal City," which combines Baudelaire's cityscape, Dante's Dis, post-war London, and fourth-century Mylae. The same desperation and turmoil that characterize the overlapping of the historical and geographical locations apply as well to a succession of historical centres of power: "Jerusalem Athens Alexandria / Vienna London / Unreal" (375–77). While the Cumaean Sibyl shows this to a lesser degree, Tiresias demonstrates the transhistorical and transpersonal anguish of one who suffers both in postwar London and in "Thebes below the wall" (245). The conflation of Lil, her " friend," and Ophelia also collapses past and present despair, and the image that floats through time is that of the selfish and self-destructive Coriolanus. In *The Waste Land*, the world of the Buddha, the Carthage of Saint Augustine, and the present all experience a corresponding "burning." Finally, this conflation of historical periods, locations, and subjects corresponds with what Eliot described as Joyce's "mythic method" of "manipulating a continuous parallel between contemporaneity and antiquity" (483). Such a technique, which Eliot affirms is a "disciplined" method that "is simply a way of controlling, of ordering, of giving shape and significance to the immense panorama of futility and anarchy which is contemporary history," applies to this poem as well as to Joyce's novel (483). In *The Waste Land*, this method subverts any humanistic or utopian ideals of progress, as the work develops a parallel "between contemporaneity and antiquity" as corresponding "panoramas of futility and anarchy."

Eliot's poem, like other Dada texts, does not just register disillusionment with ideals like humanism, utopianism, and progress; it actively brings those once-"sacred" fundamentals into question. The poem's relentless ironies of a suicidal Sibyl, April as the cruellest month, and Osiris as the pulp-crime-novel victim subvert what we could call Aldington's sacra of human dignity and nobility. The final section of the poem reinforces this reversal, as the image of a self-destructive Coriolanus replaces the altruistic call for giving alms, sympathizing, and exercising control. The poem's depiction of sexuality, which includes Lil's abortions, the rendezvous of Sweeney, Mrs. Porter, and her daughter, allusions to Tereus's rape of Philomela, the laments of the Thames maidens, and the conflation of violence and empty eroticism in the encounter between the typist and the clerk further subverts any humanistic ideals. Elements of *The Waste Land*'s survey of sordid sexuality correspond with conflation of machinery and sexuality in Picabia's "Amorous Parade," as when Tiresias describes the "violet hour, when the eyes and back / Turn upward from the desk, when the human engine waits / Like a taxi throbbing waiting" (215–17). Yet, where Picabia playfully subverts perspective, sexuality; and the fetishistic appeal of machinery, *The Waste Land*'s abortive, violent, and empty sexuality projects a permanent transition that lacks any fulfilling pleasure, any redemptive renewal or birth, as well as any centralized truths, transcendence, or telos [vision of a final goal].

Works Cited

Aldington, Richard, "The Influence of Mr. James Joyce." *English Review* 32 (1921): 333–41.

Bloom, Harold. *The Anxiety of Influence: A Theory of Poetry*. London: Oxford UP, 1975.

Calinescu, Matei. *Five Faces of Modernity: Modernism, Avant-Garde, Decadence, Kitsch, Postmodernism*. Durham, NC: Duke UP, 1987.

Camfield, William. *Francis Picabia: His Art, Life, and Times*. Princeton: Princeton UP, 1979.

Chinitz, David. "T. S. Eliot and the Cultural Divide." *PMLA* 110.2 (1995): 236–47.

Dante. *Inferno*. Trans. John Ciardi. New York: Penguin, 1954.

Davidson, Harriet. *T. S. Eliot and Hermeneutics*. Baton Rouge: Louisiana State UP, 1985.

Eliot, Thomas Stearns. "Ulysses, Order, and Myth." *Dial* 75.5 (1923): 480–83.

———. *The Complete Poems and Plays, 1909–1950*. New York: Harcourt Brace, 1971.

———. *The Letters of T. S. Eliot*. Ed. Valerie Eliot. Vol. 1. San Diego: Harcourt Brace, 1988.

Hargrove, Nancy. "The Great Parade: Cocteau, Picasso, Satie, Massine, Diaghilev—and T. S. Eliot." *Mosaic* 13.1 (1998): 83–106.

Hay, Eloise Knapp. *T. S. Eliot's Negative Way*. Cambridge, MA: Harvard UP, 1982.

Richter, Hans. *Dada: Art and Anti-Art*. London: Thames and Hudson, 1965.

Pound, Ezra. "Kongo Roux." *391* July 1921. Rpt. In Sanouillet, Michel. *391 revue publicee de 1917 a 1924 par Francis Picabia*. Paris: Le Terrain Vague, 1960. 106.

Sieburth, Richard. "Dada Pound." *South Atlantic Quarterly* 83.4 (1984): 44–68.

Silver, Kenneth. *Esprit de Corps: The Art of the Parisian Avant-Garde and the First World War, 1914–1925*. London: Thames and Hudson, 1989.

Tzara, Tristan. "Dada Manifesto 1918." *The Dada Painters and Poets: An Anthology*. Ed. Robert Motherwell. Cambridge, MA: Belknap, 1951. 76–82.

Turner, Victor. "Liminal to Liminoid in Play, Flow, and Ritual." *Rice University Studies* (1974): 53–92.

Wright, Anne. *Literature of Crisis, 1910–1922*. London: Macmillan, 1984.

THOMAS DILWORTH ON SEX BETWEEN THE TYPIST AND THE YOUNG MAN

Out of the window perilously spread
Her drying combinations touched by the sun's last rays,
(lines 224–25)

In what may be the least obtrusively allusive episode in Eliot's poem and, perhaps for that reason, the most memorable, Tiresias witnesses "the typist home at teatime" (line 222) having meaningless sex with "the young man carbuncular" (231). The young man acts merely as an agent of lust, not as an emotionally and morally complete person. This may account for the absence of a subject in sentences in which he acts: "Endeavours to engage her in caresses" (237) and "Bestows one final patronising kiss" (247). Owing to the nature of his motivation, he does not even merit a pronoun. And "she is bored and tired" (236), not even an agent of lust. The word "indifference" (242) sums up her feelings. Emotionally, psychologically, and spiritually, both of these people are mechanical: he, equivalent—before the sexual act, at least—to "a taxi throbbing waiting" (217), and she, merely an extension of her typewriter or her gramophone as she "smoothes her hair with automatic hand" (255). Except for the significance of the absent pronouns, all this has been appreciated by interpreters of the poem. But one significant word in this episode has gone unnoticed by interpreters, a word half-hidden by humble service as an adverb. It occurs in the apparently innocuous statement that the typist's "drying combinations" are "perilously spread" out her window (224–25)—"perilously," because wind might dislodge and blow away clothing drying on a clothesline out her window. In this poem, "perilously" is a word of profound literary association.

In a poem whose title refers to Malory's "waste land," the word "perilously" must evoke Chapel Perilous, the most horrific place in Malory. In part V of Eliot's poem, Malory's Chapel Perilous is reduced to a symbol of meaninglessness: "the empty chapel, only the wind's home," a place of "tumbled graves" where "the grass is singing" (387–90). The image of wind and the word "home" link this description with the typist's bed-sitter. The wind, which is at "home" in the chapel, is the cause of peril at the typist's "home" (222). In part V, the chapel is described but not named. In a sense, it has already been named in the adverb "perilously." The word identifies the empty sexuality of the typist and her visitor with one of the poem's primary symbols of meaninglessness. It is a symbol also of the absence of meaning, since a chapel ought to have value, and this one does not. It is not even, as it is in Malory, a place of terror to test the courage of a Lancelot. Expectation of meaning intensifies meaninglessness.

This is also true of sex, which, in Western culture, traditionally has psychological, cultural, and spiritual significance. It symbolizes love, happiness, vitality, fertility, and communion with God. The scriptural image for this last is the wedding between God and humanity. The theological hope is based on the widely shared sexual hope for ordinary love and happiness. The absence of all such positive meaning makes the sexual act of the typist and young man more harrowing. Indifferent sex is the real Chapel Perilous of the modern Waste Land, an act devoid of meaning and—if we, unlike the typist and her young man, want meaning—profoundly disappointing.

As "the wind's home" where "the grass is singing" the empty chapel also resonates with two other passages in the poem. One of these is the arid conversation—actually a combination of monologues, one spoken, the other interior and silent—between the upper-class couple in the over-decorated boudoir. The woman complains of "wind under the door" and asks "What is the wind doing?" (118–19). As she brushes her hair, it is like the singing grass of Chapel Perilous: "under the brush, her hair / Spread out in fiery points / Glowed into words, then would be savagely still" (108–10). The static electricity of her dry hair—in contrast to the "wet" hair of the hyacinth girl (38)—suggests infertility. It also has its counterpart in a surrealistic expression of infertility in part V: "A woman drew her long black hair out tight / And fiddled whisper music on those strings" (378–79). The passage goes on to describe "bats with baby faces," which suggest aborted fetuses and the arid intercourse of flaccid "upside down [...] towers" and "empty cisterns and exhausted wells" (383–85)—"empty" like the chapel. These passages extend and intensify the association of loveless sexuality with "the empty chapel, only the wind's home."

In its references to Hindu scriptures, the New Testament, and *The Tempest* (where Ferdinand's "sea change" corresponds to Prospero's conversion from vengeance to forgiveness), *The Waste Land* is a poem of the possibility of positive change. The reader may remember that, in Malory, Chapel Perilous is close to the Grail Castle, where the right questions asked can heal the Fisher King and make fruitful the Waste Land. So it may also be true that sex, even when meaningless as in this poem, is nevertheless somehow proximate to the kinds of love and meaning it traditionally symbolizes—near but requiring change of place, symbolizing personal metamorphosis. The chapel is "only the wind's home," and "the wind" disturbed the woman in her boudoir, but the reader may recall the symbolism of wind in the scriptural account of Pentecost, where the Holy Spirit is an agent of positive change.

Work Cited
Eliot, T. S. *Selected Poems*. London: Faber, 1954.

Camelia Elias and Bent Søerensen
on the Influence of Ovid

What at first sight might seem to be a superlative instance of the lexical fragment occurs in the following lines: "So rudely forc'd / Tereu" (206–07). The word "Tereu" appears to be an incomplete rendition of the proper name "Tereus." There is, however, another way reading "Tereu," a possibility we will explore in the following analysis. The word "Tereus" originates in Greek and belongs to a class of words ending in a digamma (a "w"). It therefore has an unusual conjugation pattern in Latin: Nominative: Tereus; Vocative: Tereu; Accusative: Terea; Dative: Terei; Genitive: Tereos. What we are dealing with in the case of Eliot's "Tereu," then, is clearly a word identical to the complete form of the vocative in Latin. (Indeed, a footnote to the text in the Norton Critical Edition flatly states this to be a vocative.) In Ovid's *Metamorphoses* we find in Liber Sextus an example of the vocative form of Tereus in a parenthetical remark by Philomela and Procne's father, Pandion, to the barbarous Tereus: "voluisti tu quoque, Tereu" ("as indeed you also desired, o Tereus"; a frequently used method of representing the vocative in English is to render it as an apostrophe—"o Tereus").

The fact that Eliot capitalizes the word strengthens the argument that Tereu is a form of a proper name, and we might suggest this occurrence in Ovid as a potential direct intertext for Eliot. However, in the facsimile edition (Eliot 1971, 43) the line originally read "Tereu tereu," the second occurrence is not capitalized. It could therefore be argued that the first "Tereu" is capitalized solely because it is the first word of a new line (thus neither of the two need be read as a proper name).

(...)

Let us now examine "Tereu" as onomatopoeia. To do so we return to the Philomela myth. We know—from several Greek sources (chiefly Apollodorus, likely building on a now lost tragedy by Sophocles), via Ovid and Shakespeare's Titus Andronicus, and from numerous other more recent treatments of the myth (Mathew Arnold's poem "Philomela" and Timberlake Wertenbaker's play *The Love of the Nightingale*, to name but two)—that Tereus rapes and mutes Philomela, who, after much suffering, manages to point to Tereus as the guilty party and to revenge herself on him by helping her sister Procne cook and serve his own son to him. Fleeing Tereus's wrath, Philomela is then transformed into a bird (often Ovid is mistakenly retold as making Philomela a nightingale, but actually it is Procne who becomes a nightingale, whereas Philomela becomes a [mute] swallow) whose song is doomed to repeat the name of her rapist. The name is not surprisingly rendered as a vocative, usually repeated and served as an exclamation, thus: "tereu! tereu!"

In Elizabethan poetry, the myth of Philomela and Tereus is often referred to via a rendition of the nightingale's vocative, in an onomatopoeic representation of its song—Twit, twit; jug, jug; tereu, tereu—creating a delightful pun on the English phrase "to rue," (that is, to regret your sins). The nightingale thus exhorts her rapist to rue the day of his crime through eternity. We find this in John Lyly's "Alexander and Campaspe" (1564):

WHAT bird so sings, yet so does wail?
O 'tis the ravish'd nightingale.
Jug, jug, jug, jug, tereu! she cries. (1–3)

Similarly we read in "An Ode" by Richard Barnfield:

Every thing did banish moan,
Save the nightingale alone.
She, poor bird, as all forlorn,
Lean'd her breast up-till a thorn,
And there sung the dolefull'st ditty,
That to hear it was great pity.
"Fie, fie, fie," now would she cry,
"Tereu, tereu," by and by. (7–14).

There is obviously good reason to think that Eliot's use of the word comes directly from these intertexts and that he preserved the word in its vocative case because it served his purpose in this section of *The Waste Land*, which is saturated through and through with the vocative mode. A glance at the page in question in the facsimile edition illustrates this fact—Ezra Pound comments twice in his marginalia: "Vocative?" and "Vocative??"

The first occurrence of "tereu" in the facsimile edition of *The Waste Land* is, as mentioned above, in fact a double: "Tereu tereu," which further strengthens our suspicion that Eliot quotes directly from Barnfield here, as opposed to Lyly's single "tereu!" We note, of course, that in the facsimile the phrase recurs and thus becomes refrain-like. Pound struck out this repetition, and it did not appear in the published first edition. The reference to the swallow, which indicates that Eliot at least got his Ovid right, was moved to line 428. Further editing also expunged a further fragmented form ("Ter"), which, unlike "Tereu," cannot be explained as merely as conjugation of "Tereus."

To read "Tereu" as a fragment, one would have to explicate the symbolic function of the word within the text as follows: The excised tongue of the nightingale cannot speak in whole words, as it is not itself whole anymore. Further, the first excision of a letter/sound is that of the sibilant, final "s," which corresponds exactly to that part of the name "Tereus" and requires a tongue to pronounce. We thus might propose that "Tereu" functions as a phonetic fragment. However, the more radical excision resulting in "Ter" cannot, of course, be explained solely as a matter of phonetic inability caused by the lack of a tongue, but perhaps could be seen as a more radical excision that leaves only the root (radix) of both tongue and word in the nightingale's mouth.

Note
1. All references to the Norton edition (2001), unless otherwise noted.

Works Cited

Altieri, Charles. "Eliot's Impact on Twentieth-Century Anglo-American Poetry." *The Cambridge Companion to T. S. Eliot.* Ed. A David Moody. Cambridge, UK: Cambridge UP, 1994.

Ashbery, John. *Reported Sightings: Art Chronicles 1957–1987.* Ed. David Bergman, New York: Knopf, 1989.

Barnfield, Richard. "An Ode." *Richard Barnfield: The Complete Poems.* Ed. George Klawitter. Selinsgrove, PA: Susquehanna University Press, 1990.

Davidson, Harriet. "Improper Desire: Reading *The Waste Land.*" *The Cambridge Companion to T. S. Eliot.* Ed. A David Moody. Cambridge, UK: Cambridge UP, 1994.

Eliot, T. S. *The Waste Land and Other Poems.* London: Faber & Faber, 1940.

———. *The Waste Land. A Facsimile and Transcript of the Original Drafts,* Including the Annotations of Ezra Pound. Ed. Valerie Eliot. London: Faber & Faber, 1971.

———. *The Waste Land. A Norton Critical Edition.* Ed. Michael North. New York, London: W. W. Norton, 2001.

Lyly, John. *Complete Works of John Lyly.* Ed. R. Warwick Bond. London: Oxford University Press, 1993.

Ovid. *Metamorphoses.* Available at <http://www.gmu.edu/departments/fld/CLASSICS/ovid.met6.html>.

Works by T. S. Eliot

Poetry

Prufrock and Other Observations, 1917

Ara Vos Prec, 1919. Republished in the U.S. as *Poems*, 1920

The Waste Land, 1922

Poems 1909–1925 (includes "The Hollow Men"), 1925

Ash-Wednesday, 1930

Anabasis, a Poem by St-John Perse (Eliot translation), 1930

Collected Poems 1909–1935 (includes "Burnt Norton"), 1936

Old Possum's Book of Practical Cats, 1939

East Coker, 1940

The Dry Salvages, 1941

Little Gidding, 1942

The Complete Poems and Plays, 1909–1950, 1952

Collected Poems, 1909–1962, 1963

Prose Criticism

The Sacred Wood, 1920

Homage to John Dryden, 1924

For Lancelot Andrewes, 1928

Selected Essays 1917–1932, 1932

The Use of Poetry and the Use of Criticism, 1933

After Strange Gods (1933 lectures at the University of Virginia), 1934

Essays Ancient and Modern, 1936

The Idea of a Christian Society, 1939

Notes Towards the Definition of Culture, 1948

On Poetry and Poets, 1957

Plays

Sweeney Agonistes (in *Criterion*), 1926

The Rock: A Pageant Play, 1934

Murder in the Cathedral, 1935

The Family Reunion, 1939

The Cocktail Party, 1949

The Confidential Clerk, 1954

The Elder Statesman, 1959

Posthumous Publications

The Waste Land: A Facsimile and Transcript of the Original Drafts Including the Annotations of Ezra Pound, 1971

Inventions of the March Hare: Poems 1909–1917, 1996

Annotated Bibliography

Ackroyd, Peter. *T. S. Eliot*. London: H. Hamilton, 1984.

A survey of Eliot's life and career.

Cuddy, Lois A. and David H. Hirsch. *Critical Essays on T. S. Eliot's* The Waste Land. Boston: G.K. Hall & Co., 1991

A collection of 24 essential essays on *The Waste Land* concerning both criticism and publishing history, beginning with Edmund Wilson's 1922 review of the poem in *The Dial*, and including essays by Conrad Aiken, I. A. Richard, R. P. Blackmur, Philip Rahv, and Cleanth Brooks. The editors' introductory essay provides a history of critical approaches to the poem.

Grant, Michael, ed. *T. S. Eliot: The Critical Heritage*, 2 vol. London: Routledge & Kegan Paul, 1982.

Collects contemporary reviews of Eliot's poetry and plays.

Litz, A. Walton, ed. *Eliot in His Time: Essays on the Occasion of the Fiftieth Anniversary of* The Waste Land. Princeton: Princeton University Press, 1973.

A collection of eight essays in which scholars, among them Hugh Kenner, Richard Ellmann, Helen Gardner, Donald Davie, and Robert Langbaum, consider the poem in light of its time, its manuscript history, its allusions, and its structure.

Rainey, Lawrence. "Eliot among the Typists: Writing *The Waste Land*." *Modernism/Modernity*, 12:1 (Jan 2005), pp. 27–84.

Rainey interweaves a careful examination of the original manuscript drafts of *The Waste Land* with a discussion of the role and the image of working women and, especially, typists, at the time the poem was written.

Schwarz, Robert L. *Broken Images: A Study of* The Waste Land. Lewisberg: Bucknell University Press, 1988.

Schwarz offers a comprehensive line by line reading of the poem, interweaving commentary, interpretation, and extensive quotation from works Eliot used as sources for quotation and allusion.

Tate, Allen, ed. *T. S. Eliot: The Man and His Work*. New York: Delacorte Press, 1966.

Tate edits a retrospective symposium. This anthology includes personal reminiscence and criticism by 26 critics.

Contributors

Harold Bloom is Sterling Professor of the Humanities at Yale University. He is the author of 30 books, including *Shelley's Mythmaking*; *The Visionary Company*; *Blake's Apocalypse*; *Yeats*; *A Map of Misreading*; *Kabbalah and Criticism*; *Agon: Toward a Theory of Revisionism*; *The American Religion*; *The Western Canon*; and *Omens of Millennium: The Gnosis of Angels, Dreams, and Resurrection*. *The Anxiety of Influence* sets forth Professor Bloom's provocative theory of the literary relationships between the great writers and their predecessors. His most recent books include *Shakespeare: The Invention of the Human*, a 1998 National Book Award finalist; *How to Read and Why*; *Genius: A Mosaic of One Hundred Exemplary Creative Minds*; *Hamlet: Poem Unlimited*; *Where Shall Wisdom Be Found?*; and *Jesus and Yahweh: The Names Divine*. In 1999, Professor Bloom received the prestigious American Academy of Arts and Letters Gold Medal for Criticism. He has also received the International Prize of Catalonia, the Alfonso Reyes Prize of Mexico, and the Hans Christian Andersen Bicentennial Prize of Denmark.

Neil Heims is a freelance writer, editor and researcher. He has a Ph.D in English from the City University of New York. He has written on numerous authors including John Milton, Arthur Miller, William Shakespeare, Albert Camus, and J. R. R. Tolkien.

Eleanor Cook is Professor Emerita, Department of English, University of Toronto. Her essays have appeared in publications such as *American Literature, Daedalus, ELH*, and *Essays in Criticism*, and *Philosophy and Literature*. Her books include volumes on Robert Browning and Wallace Stevens, as well as *Against Coercion: Games Poets Play*, and *Enigmas and Riddles in Literature*.

Louis Menand is the Robert M. and Anne T. Bass Professor of English and American Literature and Language at Harvard

University. He is a regular contributor to *The New Yorker* and *the New York Review of Books*. Among his publications are *Discovering Modernism: T. S. Eliot and His Context*, *The Metaphysical Club*, and *American Studies*.

Sandra M. Gilbert is Professor of English at the University of California, Davis. Her most recent publications include *Wrongful Death: A Memoir* (1995) and *Ghost Volcano: Poems* (1995), as well as *The Norton Anthology of Literature by Women: the Traditions in English*, 2nd edition (co-edited with Susan Gubar, 1996). The present essay is drawn from her book-in-progress entitled *The Fate of the Elegy: History, Memory, and the Mythology of Modern Death*.

Michael Levenson, Professor of English at the University of Virginia, is the author of *A Genealogy of Modernism* (1984) and *Modernism and the Fate of Individuality* (1991)—both from Cambridge University Press—and co-author of *The Spectacle of Intimacy* (Princeton University Press, 2000). He has recently edited the *Cambridge Companion to Modernism* (Cambridge University Press, 1998).

Juan A. Suárez teaches American Literature at the University of Murcia, Spain. He is the author of *Bike Boys, Drag Queens, and Superstars: Avant-Garde, Mass Culture, and Gay Identities in the 1960s Underground Cinema* (1996) and *Popular Modernism: Noise and the Reinvention of the Everday*.

Shawn R. Tucker is an assistant professor of interdisciplinary studies at Elon University in Elon, North Carolina. He holds a Ph.D. in humanities from Florida State University, and his research focuses on both early-twentieth-century modernism and humanities pedagogy.

Thomas Dilworth is the Killam Fellow in the Department of English at the University of Windsor. He is the author of *The Shape of Meaning in the Poetry of David Jones*, and editor of

Jones's illustration of *The Rime of the Ancient Mariner*. He has written numerous chapters and articles covering a wide range of poets.

Camelia Elias teaches at Aalborg University in Denmark. In addition to having published numerous articles, she has also edited two volumes of *Cultural Text Studies*, and published a volume entitled *The Fragment: Towards a History and Poetics of a Performative Genre*.

Bent Søerensen teaches at Aalborg University in Denmark, and has edited several volumes of *Cultural Text Studies*. His articles have appeared in numerous publications including *Comparative Critical Studies, Orbis Litterarum, Literary Research*, and *The Explicator*.

Acknowledgments

Cook, Eleanor. "T. S. Eliot and the Carthaginian Peace." *English Literary History* 46 (1979): pp. 341–355. © 1979 by The Johns Hopkins University Press. Reprinted with permission of The Johns Hopkins University Press.

Menand, Louis. "Problems About Texts." *Discovering Modernism: T. S. Eliot and His Context.* New York: Oxford University Press, 1987, pp. 75–94. © 1987 by Oxford University Press. Reprinted by permission of Oxford University Press.

Gilbert, Sandra M. "'Rats' Alley': The Great War, Modernism, and the (Anti)Pastoral Elegy." *New Literary History: A Journal of Theory and Interpretation* 30:1 (Winter 1999), pp. 179–201. © New Literary History, University of Virginia. Reprinted with permission of The Johns Hopkins University Press.

Levenson, Michael. "Does The Waste Land Have a Politics?" *Modernism/Modernity* 6:3 (Sept 1999), pp. 1–13. © by The Johns Hopkins University Press. Reprinted with permission of The Johns Hopkins University Press.

Suárez, Juan A. "T. S. Eliot's *The Waste Land*, the Gramophone and the Modernist Discourse Network." *New Literary History:* 32:3 (Summer 2001), pp. 747–768. © New Literary History, University of Virginia. Reprinted with permission of The Johns Hopkins University Press.

Tucker, Shawn R., "*The Waste Land*, Liminoid Phenomena, and the Confluence of Dada." This article originally appeared in *Mosiac*, a journal for the interdisciplinary study of literature, Vol 34, Issue 3, pp. 91–110.

Dilworth, Thomas. "Eliot's *The Waste Land*." *The Explicator* 61:1 (Fall 2002) pp. 43. Reprinted with permission of the Helen Dwight Reid Educational Foundation. Published by Heldref

Index

Characters in literary works are indexed by first name (if any), followed by the name of the work in parentheses